LIVE & LEARN

also by the author

NOVELS

Evangeline, The Seer of Wall St.
(historical fiction)

The Seventh Ritual, A Race for Survival
(adult thriller)

My Watch Doesn't Tell Time
(young adult)

Don't Be Afraid of Heaven
(young adult)

Fear Ain't All That
(middle grade)

Just Say Mikey
(middle grade)

SCREENPLAYS

Evangeline
(historical drama)

The Seventh Ritual
(thriller)

LIVE & LEARN
A Retiree's Guide to Keep Going

Clint Adams

Credo *Italia*

published by

Credo *Italia*
748 S. Meadows Pkwy., Ste. A-9, Box 281
Reno, NV 89521 USA

This is a work of nonfiction. All the events are true to the best of the author's recollection. Some names and identifying characteristics have been changed to protect the identity of certain parties. The views expressed in this book
are solely those of the author.
This publication is meant as a source of valuable information for the reader, however it is not meant as a substitute for direct expert assistance. If such level of assistance is required, the services of a competent professional should be sought.
The author and publisher specifically disclaim all responsibility for any liability, loss of risk, personal or otherwise, that is incurred therefore directly or indirectly, of the use and application of any contents of this book.

Copyright © 2024 by Clint Adams

All rights reserved. No part of this book may be reproduced or used in any manner without written permission of the copyright owner except for the use of brief quotations in a book review.

ISBN 979-8-9899887-0-9, 978-1-0882-8452-0 (paperback)
ISBN 979-8-9899887-1-6 (hardcover)
ISBN 979-8-9899887-2-3 (audiobook)
ISBN 979-8-9899887-3-0, 979-8-8692525-2-4 (ebook)

www.clintadams.com

To those who seek purpose

Table of Contents

ch.		pg.	
	Introduction	*i*	
		1	Ask yourself: *"Why am I here?"*
1	RE-DEFINE	*3*	
		23	Ask yourself: *"What's my purpose?"*
2	LIFE-CHANGER	*25*	
3	AFTERMATH	*41*	
4	TRUTH	*61*	
		79	Ask yourself: *"What now?"*
5	REPEATS	*81*	
6	~~PERFECTIONISM~~	*101*	
7	ACCEPTANCE	*121*	
8	GRATITUDE	*141*	
		165	Ask yourself: *"What's next?"*
9	HOPE	*167*	
10	SUCCESS	*189*	
	Acknowledgements	*iii*	
	Notes	*v*	

Introduction

Being of a certain age is a privilege. You've lived and learned (a lot) to get there. Congratulations! As retirees, you've more than likely planned for your financial security and wellbeing, but what about your personal needs? Finding a new purpose comes in a close second to financial concerns among those contemplating retirement. This book aims not only to help you cope with loss of purpose but also to discover and implement a blueprint that will keep you feeling fulfilled on a daily basis. A step-by-step process that will transform your retirement into reinvention.

Live & Learn wasn't written to change you, to make you do something differently. It's meant to re-acquaint you with something you were born with: lessons. Hands down, the greatest asset you'll possess. Your exclusive reason for being here. Told in a conversational, easy-to-read style by me, a fellow retiree, someone who's also lived and learned for a very definite purpose. My mission: to help you find value in your life lived and your life yet to be. I believe retirement is the best time of life because it's when life's lessons match life's purpose more than ever. The stories, advice, and anecdotes are all shared for you to be able to relate with ease. Absorb them strategically. The exercises give you, the reader, the chance to share, examine, and appreciate your own life's lessons and the wisdom you've gained. If you've questioned the validity of your life's worth post-retirement, here's where you'll re-discover it. Each chapter builds upon the chapter prior to teach you that you're here to live and learn.

As you approach 65, or if you're there already, pre-existing questions will become more prominent inside your mind: "Why am I here?" "What's my purpose?" "What now?" and "What's next?" These four questions make up the four sections of this book. By the time you reach "The End," you should be able to come up with your own personal answers to all four. Enjoy every moment of getting there and be grateful for the wisdom you cultivate along the way.

Happy travels!

Clint

Ask yourself:

"Why am I here?"

1

RE-DEFINE

In this chapter, you'll see value (your own). As a retiree or someone newly retired, your life may be seeking new meaning, validation, and, of course, new purpose. Here, you'll find that you've (more than likely) been living your true purpose all along. Your purpose will be renewed once it's re-defined and re-recognized. Lessons you continue to learn will have heightened meaning because you'll know they're so directly related to living your true purpose. You'll value wisdom in a different way; you've worked hard to attain it.

You'll learn by example the power of lessons lasting a lifetime. They forever change you. You'll receive tools in this chapter to help you spot these lessons quickly. In maturity, time is of the essence, but unlike your work life, no deadline is imposed. It's all up to you and your discretion. Nearing the completion of this chapter, it should be clear to you that the "why?" questions you ask will provide the greatest benefit.

Life's full of givens. No, not Robin. Remember her? A given is a known or established fact or situation; something taken for granted, a basic assumption. But who on Earth first decreed that life's purpose has anything to do with *doing*?!? And why did we accept that as a given? Attaining, achieving, acquiring, accomplishing. And those are just the *A*'s. Don't get me started on the rest of the alphabet.

Awesome if you're "on the right path." Even more commendable if you got there without the use of GPS. If you think your journey's nearing completion just because you're now retired, it's time to re-think. In the United States, the average age of retirement is 66, up from sixty years of age in the 1990s, according to a Gallup poll. Americans also live an average of 78.7 years.[1] That's a lot of time remaining. Plenty of time left to re-define your life purpose and re-commit.

No matter:
- Where you're at
- What you're afraid of
- What you're hoping for
- What you're trying to achieve
- What you're struggling with

Life's (true) purpose = *learning lessons*.

A given? When referencing most dictionaries, no. Instead, peruse your lifetime report card. If not already there, give yourself an *A+*. The best grade going, and now that you've graduated to retiree, you've earned it. No matter how long you've been out of school, you're still learning. I'm certain of it. These lessons haven't come easy because they're not supposed to.

Learning the Difficult Lessons

In your career lives, you have learned about success and failure. Both milestones, both opportunities from which to learn—about yourself. Lessons are personal; they're about you, the way you live your life, and how you relate to others. By now, you have learned the value of money; perhaps you were once wasteful and had to learn to save (a lesson to not take it for granted). The same could be said for life and death. Perhaps you had to learn the hard way to value what could easily be taken away. Maybe the love of your life came and went because you weren't emotionally available. These are challenging lessons you never asked to learn, but you got 'em anyway. They keep you going. The more lessons there are to learn, the longer you have to hang around (in life) to learn them. These lessons are why you're here. They were given to you because they're your life's purpose. Period. Full stop (if British).

As a mature adult, you wouldn't still be here if you hadn't chosen to learn from the lessons (aka challenges, obstacles, roadblocks) you've already encountered. Am I right? Quite a dull, predictable life if you hadn't. Everyone's lessons are different, unique to them, based on individual needs. Have you given thought to what yours may be? What do you feel you need to learn in this lifetime? Signing up for *Spanish 101* or *Crafting Made Easy* doesn't count. Although admirable, life and continuing education classes at your local community college are not the same. Think bigger picture.

Life's lessons have to do with you, your character in the here and now, the way you live (or don't) live your life, and the way you see and interact with others. Some examples:

- If you're impatient, you will perpetually be given lessons about the consequences of acting/re-acting impatiently. You'll be forced to slow down, whether you want to or not.
- If you're overly selfish, you'll discover that those around you will stop "giving." The imbalance will become too obvious to them. Your lesson is to realize this.
- If you're greedy, you will face an unhealthy emptiness,

always wanting more and becoming more and more empty. Your lesson is to be grateful for what you have, no matter how small.
- If you're overly critical, you're automatically pre-disposed to being sensitive or thin-skinned when facing criticism of yourself.

These lessons could last a lifetime or a short while. And, as I mentioned previously, lessons exist until the day we die, so if you feel as if you've conquered one, another will take its place. And there are usually a few others on our plates at the same time. It's too easy to just have a mere one or two. Life's challenging for a reason. So that we learn. We wouldn't grow wiser otherwise.

And sometimes, our lessons don't become fully evident for years. We don't want to have to admit we have them, we're delusional, or we're just too busy to even recognize them. In my case, it's a combination of being in denial, being humiliated, and being unaware of the truth of my own past. I recognized the easiest lessons first; then, I had to accept the reality of those most challenging.

I mention a sampling of my own lessons to learn now, early on, so you can begin the process of contemplating yours. Yours, of course, are the ones that matter most as you read ahead. In late 1991, my life changed forever. How I've lived my life in those years since (my own lessons learned) has established what I consider to be my expertise, my qualifications. Three-plus decades primarily devoted to learning my lessons, how I've benefited by having chosen to learn them, and now, passing along to you the infinite benefit(s) of lessons learned that you can apply to your own life. As I share a bit of my own history with you now, please indulge me. My lessons were and are my teacher, and by the time you finish this book, I hope you'll see yours the same way.

As I mentioned, in late December 1991, at age 34, I had an experience that transformed my life forever. A bizarre discovery of ritual abuse and murder, hidden from my memory, that had taken place in my childhood. Sounds like science fiction, but it's not. It was an unearthing of gigantic proportions, to say the least. *My* moment of truth. *The* moment in my life when I could finally say, "Now everything makes sense."

One of the byproducts of this experience was my awareness of self; this is when I began to clearly see the lessons I must learn. Patience, living truthfully at all costs, living for myself (not for others), self-love, and more than anything, compassion— compassion for others and compassion for myself. It took many years for me to admit that I was indeed a narcissist. Prior, I pointed fingers at other narcissists until I looked long and hard into the mirror. I am alive to inevitably learn that I am better than no one. My sh— *does* stink. Learning to not be a narcissist doesn't happen overnight, and there are surprising sub-lessons connected to this one.

Before going any further, what is written here is for *you*, for *your* life, and more! Some of the lessons I'll mention throughout this book are about me, my life, and my experience. They are merely examples. Only you can identify your own individual lessons, and sometimes you never will. Your purpose is not to identify; it's to learn. You may be learning lessons or not even know you've got a lesson in front of you. Be open. Be curious. And keep going. From one retiree to another, my wish is that the anecdotes in this book make you more mindful of your own lessons and help you assign meaning to each.

Much in life is defined for us. *Oxford English Dictionary* defines the noun "purpose" as *the reason for which something is done or created or for which something exists*. The definition of the verb "purpose," in formal use, is *to have as one's intention or objective*. "*Life's* purpose" is a compound noun and the *OED* doesn't define those. Up to your own individual lexicon. Perhaps not a given after all. Life's purpose is open to interpretation, just like the rest of life.

In this writing, I'll make little to no reference to "destiny" or "karma," although they could very well be linked to life's lessons. Some would say that destiny cannot be altered. This is where it's similar to lessons; we cannot order them up or schedule their arrival. You get them when you get them; there's no mixing and matching, no ordering off the menu. Most of the time, lessons show up unexpectedly (until you know better). What we do control, without question, is our desire—our decision—to learn them. We choose to, or we don't. When we realize that they are happening for a reason, they are the reason we are here, alive, it becomes infinitely easier to accept them, and once you get good at it, you no longer see them as obstacles or challenges. You see them as an organic ingredient in life. Kind of like some savory, bizarre-sounding herb you thought you'd never find tasty.

When I was a kid, I bought into the question every kid was asked, "What do you want to be when you grow up?" How horrid. Unrealistic that we could have replaced it with a much more intelligent question back then, "What do you want to learn from life?" Only in adulthood.

So, I'll ask you right here in this moment, at whatever age you're at now, "What do you want to learn from life?" Start thinking, and while you're at it, continue to erase all you'd previously thought of as (your) life's purpose. All you'd accomplished (or not), all you'd achieved (or not), any advanced position you've risen to (or not). Most importantly, all you've dreamt of happening that may or may not have materialized. How awesome to dream, accomplish, achieve, and advance. Takes a lot of time, energy, creative thought, and fortitude to make happen, no doubt about it. Congratulations to you! Job well done.

Still, beating cancer, bringing peace to the world, becoming CEO of a *Fortune* Top Ten, or bedding your fantasy lover may be connected to your purpose in life, but as standalones, they are *not* your life's purpose. The reason it's important to hammer this thought into your brain now is you're transitioning from the working world to your "rest of life." Inspiration doesn't come easy, and this is when inspiration is needed most—in your 50s, 60s, 70s, and more and more. Time moves quickly and—without warning—can come to an end.

This makes me think back to the late 1990s when I held two friends very close to me. Katherine, a co-worker of mine at a publishing company in Monterey, California, and Sean. Katherine and I would walk and talk on the beach after work, and one day, she told me she'd met someone incredible, Sean, a man she was becoming close to. I was thrilled for her. And after I met Sean, I became ecstatic. How wonderful for Katherine. How wonderful for Sean. Their marriage took place close to Sean's fiftieth birthday, and I remember asking him, "So, how does it feel? About to turn 50?" I don't recall his answer verbatim, but the gist stuck with me forever. "Fifty is when people start to die."

Only a few years after saying that, Sean died in his early fifties. Sean's kindness and compassion were off the charts; he was forever giving to others. His goodness was obvious to behold. Was Katherine shortchanged? Was she blessed by having been with Sean at all? In my opinion, it was a union that was meant to be. Fleeting in duration, filled with lessons only the two can learn from.

Watch what you say because we're lasting longer than we used to. And there's more of us lately. America's older population has grown by 38 percent since 2010, compared to an increase of just 2 percent for those under 65.[2]

Do you ever recognize "meant-to-be's"? Events that happen for a reason you presume was meant to be? Does it inevitably make the accident, the challenge, the lesson easier to accept? So different from life's lessons we learned as kids, right?
- Don't run downhill on a slippery sidewalk, or else…
- Don't drink scalding hot cocoa, or else…
- Don't walk barefoot where there's broken glass, or else…

Correct answer: Yes. Very different. Lessons you were given as a child were for your safety and survival. As mature adults, we've been there. Done that. Any lessons we learn now are for the sake of gaining and building wisdom.

Mature adults *are* survivors! *All* mature adults. Right?!? Who hasn't had struggles by this point? Struggled big time. *Everyone!* So, it's time to own that and move on.

Now that we're all admitted ~~strugglers~~ overcomers, let's aim to reduce one menace while we're at it. OK? Go. Expectation(s). Expectations that are born from perceived "purpose-driven" accomplishments. Oh, those inflexible dreams we have/had. Goals that originated decades ago that we still hold onto. Why? Are you kidding me?

So many problems we have today stem from expectations, unrealistic or otherwise. Big problems. That toxic yet delusional feeling that lives inside the pit of our senior guts, telling us that we never lived up to our potential. The worst are those that are connected to attaining anything material or tangible. Senior self-worth measured by a raise in income that never came. Living with prolonged lament over "lost opportunities." Waiting and waiting and waiting to attain something you were maybe never meant to own in the first place. All that wasted time.

Taking full responsibility for your destiny is a noble action, especially when life's lessons are unavoidable. When we see our purpose as being connected to lessons learned, there are no expectations. (For the most part) lessons are perceived as being intangible, not material, and come to us as an opportunity to learn, a gift you can't exchange. We don't spend our lives hungrily seeking them out. If you do, hats off, but make sure to have some fun while you're at it.

Well, are we having fun yet? No need to answer just now. A better question: Is even the tiniest part of you looking at the term "life's purpose" differently? Has the dictionary inside your head revised its definition, or at the very least classified it under a new sub-heading? Please continue to be open, maybe even curious, and together, let's hope.

Never Too Late to Start Over

Starting from scratch is always an option, except when it comes to lessons learned (your life's purpose). Who'd want to do that?! Don't forget that lessons are cumulative. They add up and change throughout your life—even disguising themselves to catch you off guard. Some of them, if learned completely (as infrequently as that happens), disappear altogether. How many of you have ever said, "Whew! I'm glad I don't have to live through that again." Well, when lessons are fully learned, you never will. You move on to the next or simply move on.

But, yes, getting second, third, thirty-third chances to begin again at something, anything, to get it right this time, is awesome. I'll go for that. I love it, actually. It's never too late for anything as long as you keep replacing your batteries. Batteries keep you young.

Have you ever been asked, "Would you ever want to go back to a time in your youth?" Think about your answer. It means you'd have to unlearn all those lessons, all those challenging times where you chose to learn something from adversity. Me: "Hell to the no!" I ain't going backwards for nothin'. Yes, I'd be thinner, have fewer wrinkles, and have enough hair to grow bangs again. Life is tough. Lessons are tougher. But life gets better when you know you're living it for a purpose. Your life's purpose.

Can I be honest with you? For many years since turning 34 (my life-changing experience), I saw life as a burden. For the most part, I closed myself off and took my life all too seriously. I fully accepted life as something that had to be done, something obligatory. I felt for sure that life's purpose was solely to learn lessons, and that's that. My huge mistake was to neglect the rest of what life has to offer.

There's an ecstasy to when you "get it," too. Nothing like it in the world when you end up learning when you weren't expecting to. I'd like to share a story with you, and if you ever spend too much time in your head (like I did), perhaps you'll learn to look out.

Please indulge me for a moment, and while doing so, imagine your imperfect self in this scenario. Only two years ago, a very valuable lesson came my way (again), one I'll remember forever. It wasn't a new one at all, only newly delivered and re-wrapped. Please also think of the lessons that have come your way as I share. Ask yourself, "Anything similar to me? My life? My circumstances? My opportunities to learn?"

Picture it. A two-mile trek on a dirt trail through the forest filled with streams and wildflowers. A walk that ends at the east shore of Lake Tahoe, Nevada. A place I will cherish forever. Maybe you have a similar place you consider to be your very own.

All my walks are alone, time to myself. At the end of the walk, there's a bench on the shore, with the sand under my feet and a few beachgoers in front of me. I love to be there, to sit on that bench for ten or so minutes.

While I sit alone on my bench, a man approaches me. It

looks like he's going to sit on it beside me. He has a most noticeably positive spirit surrounding him. He appears to be homeless. I spot his filled shopping cart nearby. We chit-chat at first; the type of conversation I *least* prefer.

I forever ask a ton of questions whenever I get the chance to talk to anyone, so I did. Not intrusive, but "Are you up here in the winter as well?" My questions were pointed; I was curious. He probably knew that. He was sharp and didn't mind. He was thoroughly positive and optimistic about life. And I was impressed.

The man was always upbeat, never uttering an unkind word, never complaining. Before he sat down, the judgments inside me were going crazy. My judgments began when I realized I had seen this man once before, pushing his shopping cart in the Safeway parking lot. Judging this man before he even came up to me on the bench.

When it was time for me to continue walking, I couldn't proceed without acknowledging him and his positivity. My guard had to come down. We'd never discussed anything about the possibility of this man identifying as homeless. Seemed like it may have been irrelevant because he appeared so at peace with his life and his existence on this Earth. His pleasure in living overwhelmed me. In the most non-obtrusive way, I asked, "Have you eaten lately?" Honestly, I don't remember what his answer was. He had never asked me for a thing and didn't seem to want anything. This is why I trusted this stranger; I knew he was as genuine as anyone I had ever met.

I gave him all the cash inside my wallet. I then said, "You amaze me. I'm so grateful to you! I'm sitting on this bench feeling sorry for myself—and you. You're so positive. You're not bitter. To me, you're loving life. Thank you for talking to me. You taught me something huge today."

It pains me that I can't recall that man's name. You deserve to know who he is. On that day, he was my university, and I was his student. That wonderful man was one of the many people I had judged in life. He is one of many who helped me stop doing that. He provided two things: one of the most valuable lessons I will ever receive and one of the best memories of my life. Trying to re-tell it doesn't do him justice, nor how outstanding I felt that experience was. More than anything, I hope it makes you reflect on any similar encounter you may have had, how someone else provided you with a lesson of your lifetime. Does it? Please think back every once in a while. Nostalgia keeps us trapped, but these transformational moments are meant to be valued and appreciated. Like I said, I share stories of success and failure, so you'll acknowledge your own and value each as much as I do mine.

Again, please recognize that your lessons are *yours*. They are specific to you. You may share some of the lessons I share about myself with others. Judging, thinking you're better than someone, or feeling the need to be defensively anti-social for survival are relevant lessons to me. They're the ones I was born to learn and overcome. Don't attach yourself to these, mine.

As we go further now, please put emphasis on the "I" when I encourage you to ask yourself, "Why am *I* here?" and "What do *I* want to learn from life?" Only you know the answer, but be open to a stranger helping you get closer to it.

Until you're done reading, I'm your stranger for now. Are you with me? Now that you've become more familiar with "lessons" and their importance, do you happen to see how they just might be our purpose? A part of it? None at all? If you happened to answer, "Who the hell cares about any of this?" let's talk.

Benefits of Lessons Learned

    This is why you're here. You want to reap the rewards for all your hard work, choose to learn from life's lessons, and recognize your true life's purpose:

1. Spotting lessons and mastering them adds worth to your existence and makes you feel like you're constantly working towards a goal. Whether you're retired or not, it gives you a reason to wake up.
2. We've been conditioned to believe that our jobs, our life paths, and our career paths *are* our life's purpose. If you want to succeed at any of these three, a sense of belief, dedication, and hard work are required. The same is necessary when learning lessons.
3. Lessons provide a sense of peace. When you recognize lessons and choose to accept and maybe learn from them vs. fighting them, you'll begin to feel like you're no longer constantly going against the grain.
4. By realizing that unexpected challenges, obstacles, hindrances, and roadblocks are really lessons in disguise, they lose their wallop. Their shock value isn't as shocking as before. When the same lessons reappear time after time, they'll become quite predictable. None should come by surprise.
5. Now retired, your daily planner, once filled with meetings, tasks, and conference calls, is replaced with an internal calendar that's been there since the day you were born. Best to honor these entries first.

    Hey, you wanna know what the best thing is about ~~getting older~~ maturing? You're still young enough to try new things, but now you'll ask why. More experiences will have meaning. Maybe all of them. I'm talking about life. Yours. You feel me?

Remember, you didn't place that *A+* on your lifetime report card for no reason. You earned it because you're a mature adult who has (whether you admit it or not) chosen to learn a little something from your own life's lessons. I can make this assumption because, like I said earlier, if you have no more lessons to learn, you'll be reading this book from inside a pine box with no air holes.

And, while you're still here, think about this one. In this highly competitive world, just as you pass beyond the water cooler, no one is ever going to say, "Sheesh, can you believe how long it's taking Sheila to learn her lessons? I must have learned twenty by the time I was her age." Or "Toby and I are nothing alike. He keeps saying he's got it harder than me, but I've actually heard he's got a very small lesson."

From where I stand, pettiness exists a lot less in maturity. As we age, learn, and grow wiser, petty-mindedness loses its potency. Gossip belongs on *Bravo* and *E!*, not in real life. Leave it for the young. This is where the expression "You've got a lot to learn" comes from. Get it? Got it? Good.

Only you would know if a lesson can be fun or entertaining. Get ready to laugh out loud, though, if you believe you can outthink your lesson. How crazy is that? Taking a sharp right out of bumper-to-bumper traffic only to end up in the very same situation a mere five blocks away…in an even worse part of town. Remember, one of my lessons is patience. Shoulda known better. I just love watching Judge Judy's face when she says, "Shoulda, woulda, coulda, you moron!" Almost as profound as when she yells out, "Um is not an answer!"

Think of all those yet-to-learn lessons Judge Judy has witnessed in her courtroom over the years. Countless, I'm sure. You've read how "judging others" is a lesson that's distinct to me. Not the best thing to do, but observing others ain't such a bad activity if you want to learn. It is so easy to see in others what you don't necessarily notice about yourself, be it admirable *or* sketchy behavior. Again, not judging, observing (to perhaps learn). My story about chatting with the man on the bench at the lake is a perfect example. When I stopped judging him, I learned about him and about myself. And, when thinking about how that encounter happened exactly, I know for a fact that more than likely, I would have learned nothing had I come there with a companion, friend, walk-mate, whatever.

Clarity of life's purpose may be illuminated by observing others. Your choice to observe. But, when asking for advice (from others) about your purpose, always know that their unasked-for perspectives and points of view come with it. Be careful. Practice discretion. If you're not a fan of alone time, try it out every once in a while. I wouldn't be able to survive without it, to be sure. Go for it. In this digital climate, consider taking a vacation, maybe a long one, from social media. Social media is indeed important for business but can be so unhealthy when you're knowingly or unknowingly straying from your own sense of self.

As I've mentioned, one of my lessons is not to rely on anyone and to believe in myself first and foremost. If you feel that you give thought to the number of likes, comments, or shares your post has gotten on any social media, re-think. Relying on approval from others is deadly to those whose identities may face fragility. Instead, look in the mirror, give yourself a "like" with your thumb of choice, and rejoice.

Validating Yourself Once and For All

As a mature adult, it's time to substantiate your possibilities. Life begins when you believe in yourself and rely on no one. It also helps a lot when you can do this with zero animosity attached. Be your own pep squad. Cheer for your cause daily, knowing that the star player, the most vital participant, is you. Doubters be gone, but appreciate the fire they ignite in you. Be grateful for rejections; they inevitably make you need approval less and less. This approach is much better than traversing that windy road to Bitter-town.

Alone time puts you closer to your purpose. In the pages that follow, I'll offer a few optional exercises. These exercises are meant to be done alone, with no one else around—you and only your own perspective present. If you don't like doing homework, there's no need to do it. After all, you've already earned that *A+* long ago. Your final grade, the one for effort, comes at the end, though. No pressure.

Just to clarify, that *A+* wasn't a given. Mature individuals have undoubtedly taken action and passed more tests. They're folks who have been around the block a few times and are smart enough not to step in the pile of poop on Mrs. Finebaum's lawn. Looks like Sparky must have eaten a burrito for lunch. Sometimes, you can avoid the dog plop; sometimes, it appears in your shoe tread by surprise after the fact. Isn't that pleasant? How'd that happen?! A lesson or not, the latter shows you that for a good part of life, you're not in control. Those dried bits that remain stuck inside that deep tread may be a reminder to slow down, be careful, watch your step, pay attention, or beware of dogs that dine at Taco Bell.

Sparky's got me thinking big. About your purpose. Yes, yours. It's major, this next notion to ponder. Do you believe your life purpose (your lessons to learn) was something you were born with? Something that was given to you specifically? Deliberately? By now, we've discussed and re-defined purpose, life's purpose, lessons, and what they're for, but it's up to you as an individual to determine their origins. Go. Be fearless.

Marching to your own beat takes bravery. Bravery, combined with the other "b" word, belief, could be the winning formula to make all dreams real. An incredible concept. I've ordered both many times; sometimes they arrive, sometimes one comes in while the other doesn't, and sometimes, when tracking either, I'm routinely notified that the shipment's been delayed. Can you relate? Hard to have it all at once, ain't it?

Trust me, I have infinite respect and admiration for folks that can achieve so much. Hats off. Some folks persevere no matter what, believing in themselves and their vision without wavering. It's never good to compare yourself to others, but when you're young, perhaps it's only natural to be jealous. Again, maturity works wonders, especially when it gets you beyond yourself, seeing only what's on the surface. "Don't judge a book by its cover" is a saying that's applicable both inside and outside the card catalog.

Do you want to know where the seed was planted for the creation and development of this book? Next to a StairMaster at a gym in Cupertino, California. A few years ago, when my local gym in Santa Cruz—with frequent plumbing issues—partially flooded, I drove over the hill on Highway 17 to nearby Silicon Valley. A radically different vibe at that gym, for sure. I began my workout on an upright exercise bike like I always do and happened to begin chatting with the woman next to me climbing steps. She was newly retired and pleasant. (Maybe that's why.)

She was easy to talk to and so open when discussing her former life as a tech exec. We were on the second level with a view of the first below. She pointed out a few co-workers she was able to recognize using the weight resistance machines, not by name but by what they do. This was the impression I'd had myself as soon as I stepped into the gym. Do-ers. Big-time, successful do-ers. Kind of intimidating. For me, anyway. Made me so curious, though.

"Wow, I'm impressed," I told her. "So accomplished. A lot of them so young."

"All younger than me," I said to myself.

"You should be here at six in the morning. On the dot, they're at it," she replied. All planned out, their entire lives, so driven to succeed and climb that ladder. No time to doubt themselves or their beliefs. I could only be impressed when I wasn't noticing the dissimilarities between them and myself.

What dedication it must take. What's next, though? I asked the woman next to me because I mostly wondered what you replace that drive and determination with. I honestly don't remember, but she'd mentioned some incredible things, all having to do with doing. Good for her, I thought. My instinct told me that she craved more. Once I hit thirty minutes on the bike, I thanked the woman next to me for our conversation, and my mind continued to wander. I went downstairs and proceeded with those machines. Two reps per machine, my mind wandering in between.

That conversation had staying power. Although I took no action immediately after, when my mind was wandering once again while back at home in Santa Cruz, I consulted the Internet. My instinct was in high gear because I already knew the search results before they even came up. Keywords: spirituality, retirement, Silicon Valley. An odd combination, to say the least. I immediately found evidence for the question that had already formed in my head while at that gym: What motivates high achievers once they near retirement? My instinct told me, "This is when they begin to ask the *w*-word questions." They might ask, "After having accomplished all I ever wanted, why? Why did it all happen the way it did? What did it all mean? For what purpose? Why am I here? What's *my* purpose? What'll I do now? What's next?"

Lots. Just of a different sort. These are intelligent people, and the most intelligent people always ask why. After being so glued to their goals, perpetually hungry for more, I can only assume they want answers. I believe these people are *you*. You are bright, accomplished, and intelligent, or else you wouldn't have earned that *A+*. It was deliberate. I'm not judging you; instead, I'm sensing your needs as if feeling my own.

Retirees are hungry for more. Remember TV channels? Turning that dial clockwise? Do you recall when numbers became networks? Before broadcast television went streaming? Well, why not try out a new platform? New programming is in your future, I'm sure of it. *You: The Untold Story* airs on its own channel 24/7. A documentary? Biopic? Reality show? You decide. My wish for you is that you entertain what's prescribed in this book. Written and presented to you in a strategic order: past to present to future. Living and learning are two things you've already been doing long before retirement. Keep the momentum going. Notice all that makes you different and appreciate those nuances.

In between these ten chapters, take a moment to look in the mirror and notice all that wisdom. Chapter One divulges the most essential concept: re-defining the term "life's purpose." By the end, you'll be more aware of your own brand of success that you choose, develop, and improve. Take in all the lessons you've learned. See your life's purpose and listen to it telling you that there's more to ~~do~~ learn. You're not done by a long shot. If seeing life's purpose as "infinite lessons to learn" is a new concept to you, you're just beginning.

I hope so much that you resonate with the words written here. Creative interpretation is encouraged as you move from one chapter to the next. Feel yourself grow as you do. These words, these chapters, were written for you specifically. Absorb them—this journey—with patience and enjoy your ride replotted.

TAKE ACTION

Are you open to re-defining your own "life purpose?" It's OK if you aren't. Your words matter. Your opinions and feelings matter. They shape outcomes.

- *If you see your life's purpose as lessons to learn, what are some (of yours)?*
- *If you don't, how do you define "life purpose?"*

Please formulate your answers based on your own life, your own outlook. (For this and subsequent TAKE ACTIONs, please write only one paragraph, four to six full sentences. You can dictate this if you prefer. After completing, store away and don't discard.)

If writing resonates with you (and isn't distracting), please enter these reactions and responses into your own dedicated notebook or journal. Keep it on hand, nearby, as you make your way through this book.

Ask yourself:

"What's my purpose?"

2

LIFE-CHANGER

Here, you'll now focus on your most significant life-changing event. You'll become familiar with a few that others have experienced and how their transformations came about. As you read, reflect. Place yourself in the shoes of those whose lives have changed profoundly because of a single occurrence. As you proceed within this chapter, you may understand more why I share my personal stories. My anecdotes are my lessons, and they're told for the purpose of establishing trust via exposure. Explore the power that your own vulnerability will yield.

You're asked to analyze your life-changer. Do you feel it happened for a reason? Do you believe things are meant to be? At the end of this chapter, you'll be asked to act twice. First, identify the single, most noticeably life-changing event in your life. Second, answer the following question: Did it then, or shortly thereafter, make your lessons (life's purpose) obvious to you?

*R*etirement is a life-changer. How'd you handle it? How are you going to? It's one of the most significant transformations you'll ever undertake. But is it *the* most? Give it some thought. Life changes all the time, but everyone's got *one* life-changing moment. It's the most obvious one and can't be swapped for another. Just as you've presumably done in the past, make a list of five noteworthy times of your life when "going back to the way things were" became impossible. Study your list. Pick the item that stands out most. Then, let it go. Let time pass. Study the list again.

Pick Just One

Think about other means that may help you identify that singular moment when the course of your life changed forever. One. Examine a scrapbook. Look at old photos, journals, and calendars, but more than all else, jog your memory. Once you whittle down your top five, your true life-changing event will be a standout. Honor your selection once you've identified *the* one. You're going to find that that singular life-changing moment catapulted you into your true purpose for living.

At the time, it may've been unclear, but now, looking back at a past life-changing event/crossroads (whether you regard it as being good, bad, or in between), you'll likely see that your purpose was thrown in your face. Maybe it wasn't apparent then, but we eventually recognize this as the moment we're introduced to our true purpose, one we're aware of forever thereafter. Several can come to mind, but there's one in particular that's the biggie, the most prominent. A moment in time when everything in your life changed. This is it! This is *the* one! As an accomplished multitasker, ponder yours as you read on.

Everyone of a certain age has had a life-changer, even country-pop singer Shania Twain. At 22, when attending a computer programming class (her Plan B), Shania was informed that both her parents had been killed in a car accident. She had three younger siblings who would need her care. Shania had already been singing since she was a child, but now, she faced a "sink or swim" mentality. There was no longer room to entertain a Plan B on her calendar.

This happens to many people. It's not necessarily the life-changing event itself; it's what happens immediately after, a time when life will never be the same again. The aftermath of your own life-changing event or turning point crams purpose down your throat; it's the time that yields the truth, a new life, the new you, your true purpose. As outsiders, we can look at Shania Twain as inspiration. She's done a lot with her career, but again, we'll never know the lessons that underlie her life events.

When asked how she felt about getting nominated for Grammy awards or similar, Shania said something like, "I am grateful, but I don't let myself get excited or feel anything different than what I normally feel. When my parents died so suddenly, I know anything can change in an instant. Without warning, anything can be taken away just as easily as it came." A keen outlook and wise perspective. Now that you're a more mature, stable individual, do you allow yourself to become (too) excited? Or excited within reason?

Another life-changer and lesson I'd experienced myself but certainly applies to many: I was in Austria, staying with friends. One afternoon, my friend, his wife, and his two children chose to take me on a tour of the city of Graz. It was quite hilly. We walked up one hill where there was a well-visited, prominent vista point. We five stood there looking out at this massive sight. The raised and tilted placard before us pointed out several nearby landmarks in the distance for (us) tourists to view. When glancing down, one description caught my attention because I recognized something very familiar about it.

After glancing once more, I searched for what it was

pointing out close by. A rather large arena beyond turned out to be a football stadium. Though my German was elementary, I could readily figure out what the sign was referring to. It was pointing to the Arnold Schwarzenegger Sportzentrum. The sign read, ~~Arnold Schwarzenegger~~ Sportzentrum. His name looked as if it had been scratched over with a knife or sharp object.

"Arnold Schwarzenegger? The governor of California?" I asked.

"Yes, He's from Graz," Jannik replied.

"Look at this," I said while pointing to the vandalism.

Nodding, Jannik told me, "The death punishment." He continued, "We don't have this here. Our past." The Holocaust. Deliberate killing. Austria learned from its past. Never again.

I didn't focus too much on lessons when I visited Austria, but I knew the Holocaust was a big one, possibly the biggest, most significant life-changing event humanity will ever face. Austria certainly learned from this period, but did the rest of the world? History, lessons, repeat themselves until they are learned. Let's hope there's nothing that tops this one. Let's learn it together and stop it before it's too late. OK? You in?

If you're now pondering life-changing events that have affected you, great! We've discussed different types of events, some that are applicable to an individual and others that affect us collectively. Keep thinking of your very own life-changing event, one you'll never forget. It should be specific to you. Also, a life-changing event doesn't necessarily have to be considered challenging or negative to elicit or introduce a lesson. It could be a joyous or harmonious happening. It could also be something that happened unexpectedly or something you manifested. It's all up to you. Whatever your big, huge, once-in-a-lifetime life-changing event is, make note of it now.

Life-changing events and, more precisely, their

aftermaths, give us an instantaneous sneak peek into our true purpose, the real and true purpose we were given at birth. A colossal jumpstart. Reminders of why we're here and the lessons we were meant to learn. There are literally a million-and-one life-changing events, crossroads, turning points. But, if you're still thinking of your one and only most significant, consider these few random examples.

Negative life-changing events:
- You lost all your money in a Ponzi scheme.
- The home you lived in for thirty-plus years was destroyed by a hurricane.
- You find out your spouse/partner has been cheating on you.
- The legs you've relied on for walking suddenly become paralyzed.

Positive life-changing events:
- Your daughter marries the man/woman of her dreams.
- You just won an Oscar.
- After two years, you—suddenly—awaken from a coma.
- For the first time, you feel validated by someone.

Life-changing events you manifested:
- You left an abusive relationship.
- You moved to a foreign country and stayed there.
- You achieved twenty years of sobriety.
- You realized you didn't need validation from anyone.

There's no doubt that life-changing moments allow us to be born again. They give us the clearest picture of ourselves we could ever ask for, unfiltered and untouched. We're in the here and now. The clock never stops ticking, especially when we're using self-charging batteries.

Throw regret to the curb. The number one regret among people facing death: "I wish I'd been brave enough to live a life true to myself, not the life others expected of me."[3] Be brave *now*!

You and I and everyone in between here on Earth (maybe elsewhere, too?) are meant to be living the lives we were given when we were born. I don't know who I was in a past life, nor do I care, and I certainly can't waste time wondering what my lessons were before I was born or if they carried over into this one. Possible, but irrelevant to me right now. Do you feel the same? Time is precious, so let's get to know each other.

Getting Personal

Trigger Warning: The following material references extreme violence and ritualistic sexual abuse. Discretion is advised.

As you continue to read, think about yourself. Think about your own potent, personal story and how miraculous you feel once you open up.

Whether your life-changing event is something you want to recall always or forget about entirely, your story may be worth telling (and re-telling) if it can help someone else. My goal for you while reading this book is to learn something a bit different while living a life filled with purpose and promise. This is how I now live my life unequivocally. Without question, I know why I am here. I know my purpose; I know exactly what I was meant to learn. My lessons seldom come to me by surprise anymore.

I also want you to know more about me so you know where I'm coming from, what my backstory is, and what led me to live my life quite differently. It all began with my life-changing event. Thirty-plus years ago. Like a lifetime ago, but for you to better understand the content of this book, you deserve to know what brought me here. By the time you near the end of this book, I hope so much that I've earned your trust and that you'll be open to absorbing the honesty I've shared.

Several years ago, I stopped telling my story about my life-changing event and more. I felt that by re-telling it, I'd be keeping myself stuck to my past, preventing me from moving on. There's power in storytelling, though, and that's why I want you to tell yours. For the moment, I'll share mine. As mentioned earlier, some life-changing events are seen as good, some bad. Some are sought out, and others arrive unexpectedly. Mine was a combination of all four. It took place on December 31st, 1991, when I was 34 years old. It was something I *never* would have expected, but at the same time, I *was* seeking out the truth. At 34, what I wanted most and never had was to get close to someone, to have a relationship. All my life, I felt there was a nagging reason why I could not. In early November, my fierce determination led me on a two-month journey that consumed every second of my life, every fiber of my being. It had to. I sincerely feel that had I not discovered the truth in late December, I wouldn't be here to share these words with you right now. If you speak and live the truth, you deserve the very same back and nothing less. If you're not yet living this way, I highly recommend it. The consequences are worth it.

In early November of 1991, I happened to be in New York City to run in the marathon. My best friend at the time, a very intelligent, highly educated young woman, had been there a few weeks earlier. She knew how distraught I was at once again not being able to connect in a relationship with someone. While in Greenwich Village, she stumbled upon a psychic who gave her feelings about her own relationship issues. "Clint, you should go see her when you're there." My reply was a laugh and a shake of the head. No way. What nonsense. Not in a million…until I found myself in New York, where I continued to be so desperately sad about another relationship that did not/could not happen.

I ended up walking into the woman's lavish studio, and she instantly asked, "What do you think when I say the initial *J*?"

OMG! That's Jim. How did she know this?

"Are we ever going to get together?" I asked.

"There is a woman in your life who is extremely jealous of you. She meditates against you daily. *M*."

"Michael?"

"No, a woman."

"Mom?" It couldn't be her. I loved and trusted my mother. When I walked out, I let all go, ran the marathon with my worst time ever, and flew back home to San Francisco. I forgot all about it. Until...

I began asking questions, more questions, lots of questions that became interrogations. The more questions I asked my mother, the more my own intuition kicked in to guide me, another thing I didn't give credence to at that time. Tangible clues and my intuition and deductive reasoning led me to put together an unsolved puzzle I never knew existed. All for the purpose of finding out why I could not have a relationship.

At 34 and prior, I felt so confident. I used to be extremely sociable and was able to talk to anyone freely. Yet, way down deep, there was a very sad person inside me whose origins were about to be exposed.

Towards the very end of 1991, fierce determination and random clues (that had become blatant) led me to discover a truth I had never known: my father shot and killed Robert Smythe, his partner in the Oakland Police Department, while he, the partner, was on top of me, raping me at age two. Two shots to his head while he was on top of me.

This rape was not the first. It had been standard practice, except on this occasion, the partner had begun before my father was there to supervise. Both my parents at the time, along with

Robert Smythe, were "allegedly" involved in devil worship (today known as Satanic ritual abuse).

When I had asked my mother about the murder for the hundredth time, she blurted out something new, "He was protecting you!" From what? No elaboration ever followed, but that inadvertent slip of the tongue corroborated all. Was I about to be sacrificed back then? Had this man's impatience interrupted a shared plan?

Robert Smythe had no family. His body was buried in our backyard, and a tree was planted on top of it. The body was soon after dug up and removed. I have no idea where it went from there.

Research shows that our earliest memories form between the ages of three and four. I am grateful that I was too young to remember, but there was a "recollection" that came back to me as an adult. I'm grateful there were no more. Just that one. I don't want to ever experience it again. Near the end of 1991, in my bedroom in San Francisco, I was awakened by two loud gunshots. I bolted up from a reclined position, drenched in sweat. I saw this as validation for the facts I had been piecing together about my childhood, my past.

A therapist had once told me, "You're not meant to remember anything. Those memories could (conceivably) kill you."

On January 1st, 1992, reality set in. I was in survival mode once more, just as I had unconsciously been as a child. Not having any idea of what would come next and realizing that my mother had a set of keys to my apartment, I immediately had my locks changed. Fright and uncertainty overwhelmed me. I feared for my own safety. These new facts erased the childhood I'd known to be true. Now, I understood it to be a lie. How could I possibly trust my parents again? This began my distrust of *everyone*. Would my mother tell my father that I now knew about the murder? Would either of them cause me harm? Would my father have me killed? My mind was panic-stricken. I'd sincerely believed that there's no telling what they would do to me now that I knew of the murder.

Learning the truth explained everything; I thought it would instantaneously transform my life for the better. In a curious way, it did, merely because I had found those unimaginable answers. But then, protection mode set in. Takes forever and a day to undo.

You and I will talk about the importance of the aftermath (of life-changing events) in the next chapter, but my immediate aftermath led me to move out of my San Francisco apartment. I had been living there for thirteen years, and my mother had been paying for it. Yes, at 34, I was still incapable of being on my own and was dependent on my mother for survival. She never objected to this arrangement. Whether it was control of some sort or something else, I take full responsibility for being so weak, dependent, and perhaps even lazy.

I moved to the coastal town of Half Moon Bay, California, and was terrified most of the time, but the nature there soothed me. It took me time to accept that this was my (new) reality. After having been trim and fit during my years in San Francisco, I had gained something like one hundred pounds in just a few months in my new life. Aftermath: A protection mode that was thrust upon me. Nature's body armor that keeps others intentionally at bay.

Thirty-plus years later, about two-thirds of those one hundred pounds are gone; one-third remains, and I still have never had a relationship.

Revealing this story to you now has made me uncomfortable because there's still tension attached. I hardly ever tell it anymore, but I want to convey to you now, as I will continue to do, that there's nothing more powerful than the truth and exposing/expelling all of it. Looking back, I am grateful to have learned what I did about my past. If I hadn't, the secrecy (intentionally kept by others) would have killed me. Either way, I'm still here. Grateful.

This event gave me my purpose. Most accurately, it soon after delivered my mission of learning why and learning compassion. In these thirty years plus, I fled from narcissists (my mother, my father, nearly everyone in my life), only to find that I was one myself. I solved my own mystery, but when I began to ask myself, "What made my parents this way? What was done to them? What happened (to them)?" my life changed forever. I had begun living what I was meant to learn. The hard way, but isn't that the only way? Lessons don't come easy.

In recent years, I have done my very best not to blame others, not to point fingers, to accept, to be patient, and to know that the world does not revolve around me. Everyone suffers. And the timing's never been better (for all of us) to be made aware of this. In 2013, former President Barack Obama predicted that the consequences of America's "empathy deficit" would prove longer lasting than the federal deficit.[4] It's time to care about others.

Before December 31st, 1991, I hadn't been introspective and did not believe in God, spirituality, psychotherapy, or the power (and gift) of instinct. I thought I was just fine the way I was. Looking back, I clearly see that prior to that time, I was a child living inside a 34-year-old body. Emotionally an infant. Now, I've grown to be 66 inside and out. Can't say that's good or bad, but it's reality. And reality = the truth. Wouldn't have it any other way. Living a false life is not living at all; it is clearly not the way we were meant to be living. It would be like having your subconscious yelling out your lessons (your life's purpose) every single day and ignoring them. Constant, prolonged, self-imposed agony.

OK, enough about me. But at least now you know.

For a Reason

Do you believe that everything happens for a reason? Maybe it does, maybe it doesn't. I ~~kind of do~~ mostly believe it, but it's too simplistic to just accept it as a given. There's more to it. The rest is for you to contemplate and then elaborate upon. Not following trends—and letting them pass through unnoticed—is my preference; it always has been. There's something to not going with the grain all the time and being your own person.

A bit ago, on several occasions, I asked you to identify your life-changing event. Assuming that's been done, and whether you believe it happened for a reason or not, it's time to move beyond and ask why. If you were in elementary school right now, this is where the test prompt would read, "Please explain." So, do so. In your head, for the moment.

Scrutinize those two to six months following your "life-changing" event (if/after it's been properly identified). That's the time to focus on now. Shift to those weeks and months and try re-examining the way you lived—and made it through life—immediately after the dust settled. Think for a moment. Did your priorities shift? Did you go from "staying on schedule" to "taking better care (of yourself)?" It's usually where you move yourself to the number one position within your life, even if this doesn't last. This is when you see yourself, your life, and your purpose with no filter or camouflage.

No doubt about it: this "immediately after" time is when there's no one in the mirror but you. Just you, no one else, no story fillers, only your own. Let's review some examples.
- You're fired from your dream job →→ (Two to six months later) you discover you were being grossly underpaid.

(Ultimate) lesson: You learn that you deserve better; you

deserve what you're worth.

- JFK airport is fogged in, your flight is diverted to Philadelphia, and you miss that once-in-a-lifetime business meeting →→ (Two to six months later) you're engaged to that guy you'd met by accident at the Liberty Bell.

  (Ultimate) lesson: You learn that your long-neglected love life needed restoration; you allow yourself to open up and are healed from decades-old hurt and pain.

- Your only daughter comes out to you as a lesbian, and your preconceptions lead you two to part ways →→ (Two to six months later) you discover that she's terminally ill and wants to reunite.

  (Ultimate) lesson: You learn to accept her (and what she's all about) unconditionally.

- You're an addicted gym rat and do your daily workouts no matter what but are chronically injured and fatigued to the point that you're forced to quit →→ (Two to six months later) you find that you've lost weight, look about the same, and are much less tired.

  (Ultimate) lesson: You learn moderation and variation; you're less reliant upon the one thing you had once believed made you feel good.

Are you noticing the timeline(s) here? Ultimate lessons seem to arrive because of life-changing events. Maybe ultimate lessons appear readily, but some digestion or evolution needs to take place.

When looking back to your life-changing event, did you see signs of your true purpose emerge over time? Or was it apparent immediately?

If stress was involved, my guess is that your lesson (purpose) became apparent to you much after the fact. Life-changing events that often come with major stress attached include:

- Job loss
- Death of a loved one
- Moving
- Injury/illness
- Divorce

You have to take care of yourself physically, emotionally, and more before taking the time and luxury of seeking a deeper meaning. If you're already used to seeing your life's purpose as learning lessons from all, you'll perhaps identify the lessons sooner.

Lessons also provide healing; they provide a sense of what may have appeared as senseless. Judge Judy always says, "If it doesn't make sense, it's not true." Well, God bless her. Lessons *are* true for those who believe in them. They're meant to be, and they give us all a purpose. I have no idea what Judge Judy's lessons are, nor do I know why she changed hairstyles. Only she knows. And possibly Officer Byrd.

Putting together the "life-changing event-wellbeing-lessons" chain requires patience. Lessons take as long as they're gonna take. At the time of this writing, I'm 66. Sometimes, I need A LOT of reminding.

How about you? Do you need the same? Is patience already established in your life?

Everything's Connected

One thing leads to the next, doesn't it? Otherwise, how would Laverne DeFazio get to second base without having already gotten to first? You gotta go through the thing before you can attempt to make sense of it. This is how I see it. And you?

Question life while you're at it. Everyone has a curiosity about them. Don't be afraid to ask, and most importantly, don't be afraid to see and accept the truth. There's nothing more powerful.

If you haven't yet discovered why you're here, or what your life-changing event is, or what your lessons are, that's cool. It's early here. Let's call it "seed-planting." Something may come to you when you least expect it.

My main point at the moment is that one thing leads to another. One experience happens so we can undergo a brand new one that makes us feel better and more fulfilled than the previous (because now, there's wisdom behind it). The new experience adds richness and meaning to the old. And don't forget to see the lighter side of both.

TAKE ACTION: Part 1
Walk through the following in your head (if you feel comfortable enough to do so). This is not intended as a writing exercise, but you can write your answers if you wish.
- *In as few words and as simply stated as possible, what's your life-changing event?*
- *Take several minutes to stop and think deeply.*
- *Ruminate for a bit on your life-changing event and bring it into the present (if you feel completely safe right now).*
- *What was it? When did it happen? After you've identified it, let's move on.*

TAKE ACTION: Part 2
Writing/dictating often demonstrates proof of your thoughts and feelings. Please write or dictate answers to the following questions.
- *After time has passed beyond your life-changing event, do*

you look back and feel that it happened for a reason?
- *Do you feel that this event/this crossroads has made you more aware of your purpose in life and what you were meant to learn?*
- *If so, what's most crucial for you to learn within it? Lessons about...?*

3

AFTERMATH

Here, you'll see why aftermaths cannot exist without life-changers. Although one may last only a moment and the other may last a lifetime, both should be valued equally. Aftermaths breed wisdom. You'll be asked to measure and value yours if you haven't already. You'll be asked to scrutinize the many signs and synchronicities you've experienced in life. You'll begin to ask "why?" more than any other question.

This is where you'll also differentiate between simple cause and effect and substantial change that seems pre-destined (being connected to your purpose). You'll again learn why it's important to share vulnerabilities, and you'll aim to do the same. There's infinite power in truth. Nearing the end of this chapter, you'll be asked to think about how you view change. Do/did you embrace retirement? Do/did you resist it? Change is constant; playing the fool is optional. It's time to play.

*I*nsert two fresh new AAs, because your cordless clock's about to speed up. A lot of folks don't like to age, but in this case, it's truly a time to celebrate. The aftermath (of your life-changing event) does more than help you identify your lessons, your purpose in life. Way more. This is when the emotional life that's been dormant prior, without you even knowing, catches up to the physical. This is a good thing! It's way more than a perk.

Who on Earth wants to be living in an aging body when your insides are still juvenile (meaning little to no wisdom contained therein)? It's not fair. Wisdom comes from emotional maturity, and damn it, you've earned it! Prior to living your truest life, you've basically been a child. Algebra ain't my strong suit, but keep this equation in mind: Immediately after your life-changing event, you're gonna age (emotionally) one month per year until your physical and emotional ages match. Well, this is how it happened for me. My body and mind weren't prepared to live with the truth and its consequences until I was ready to learn from both.

Getting Caught Up (Emotionally)

This is when your life begins anew. You've graduated. You're all caught up. It's not a joy ride, because there's more work to do, because there always is. Now, you've got your purpose to live out and lessons to learn. To clarify: lessons you *choose* to learn. Prior to your life-changing event, you may have been presented with a plethora of lessons but chose to learn from none of them, sticking your tongue out at each and every one. You probably didn't know those were lessons and referred to all as one big "pain in the ass." Try a stool softener.

The immediate aftermath is no picnic. How can it be? It's where you must recognize the new you in the mirror. All those years spent as the old (immature) you, and now you've got nothing but reality to deal with. It's challenging but rewarding at the same time. You're now living the life you were meant to live. Your purpose is becoming clearer and clearer. It's never easy. But now, almost everything has meaning, and you're not living some random existence.

One of the best parts of a life lived intentionally is the ability to see clues and signs readily, if not for the very first time. They are out there constantly, repeating themselves if we're lucky enough to catch a second glimpse. Whew! Gotta be grateful for those. Clues, signs, and such are like GPS for our minds. And those cameras on the outside of our cars. All helpful alerts. They help us prevent a lot of sh—, and they create a lot of good just the same. On the other hand, they create and prevent absolutely nothing when they're ignored. They always lead us in the best direction, so it's best to respond to those indicators as soon as they appear on our internal display panels.

Something else happens once you mature after your life-changing event; you're ready for the hardest of the W-word questions. Before, you may have asked, "What?" "Where?" "Who?" and a few others, but now that you've graduated, you take on "Why?" This is where your best answers come from. Previously, you may have asked, "Why am I here?" but didn't really mean it. Now you do. You'll be glad because you've earned it. You've moved beyond talking trivia.

When you get to know someone, anyone, maybe you'll be brave enough to wonder out loud. This is the best way to understand what makes someone tick. Maybe have compassion for them and understand them on a deeper level. They'll likely appreciate the consideration that went behind your question. I always used to wish the world worked this way, for folks to look beyond the cover, the wrapping, because there's such a different story inside.

Everyone wants to be validated, and this cannot happen if you only see the surface. Make a deliberate effort to look deeper.

Awareness begets validation.

In 2018, I happened to see something that validated me greatly. It was during the time when Oprah Winfrey used to contribute to the show *60 Minutes* with a segment she created and seemed to have much passion for, having to do with treating childhood trauma. Trauma-informed care for kids. Her professional expert, Dr. Bruce Perry, talked about how early childhood trauma impacts development. To some, none of this is news, but hearing from them both gives this concept so much credibility.

Oprah said that when addressing children who express difficult behavior, it's most appropriate to ask, "What happened to you?" vs. "What's wrong with you?" She even refers to the former as being her "life-changing" question. This gives merit to the truth of the situation. It doesn't shift responsibility for actions but rather provides an explanation. In 2021, psychiatrist Dr. Perry and Oprah's book—*What Happened to You? Conversations on Trauma, Resilience and Healing*—was published and is a superb vehicle from which to learn and embrace.

Many folks judge and are judged by their covers. Taking the time to look inside takes patience. As older adults, we've got more time to step back before diving in. Again, ain't it grand being more mature? As Sarah Palin would say, "You betcha." You wanna go back? Hope not. It's not the easy out it appears to be.

The reason I mention all this is because you can't appreciate your aftermath until you decipher your beforemath. Even if you flunked math altogether, give yourself an *A* for effort right now. Being a mature adult and having the gumption to see things differently at this point in life takes courage. So does seeing and recognizing signs.

Seeing the Signs

These become most prominent immediately after your life-changing moment. Signs, clues, intangible assists. Stuff that you used to call coincidences prior to your ~~change of life~~ life-changing moment. After you had yours, did you begin to see these clues and signs that pointed you in a certain direction? To a certain course of action? Do you recognize these now? You've probably had many. They seem to work closely with lessons. Hand-in-hand. They also seem to be so directly associated with dispositions as well. When you're feeling more negative, you're gonna receive fewer helping signs and assists. But when you're even a bit more optimistic, feeling positive and grateful about your life and what's out there, a "surprise" assist seems to come your way.

People struggle! Other people struggle! They're everywhere. Notice them. Feel *their* pain. My biggest lesson of all time is learning and practicing empathy. Today, I do my best every day to acknowledge others and have compassion for them. And, at the same time, compassion for myself. Make sure you're doing the same.

Although I wasn't one of those 1000 percent overachievers at the gym in Silicon Valley, I still had high standards and aimed big. This is where acceptance comes in handy. You with me? Have you heard of it? Trust me, it solves everything. Write this down: "Acceptance is *not* synonymous with defeat or giving up!" It means you're taking a load off. Give yourself a break. There's no need to push yourself towards goals that may not even be yours in the first place.

In addition to feeling a natural compassion for others, these encounters cause me to slow down myself. The same goes for you; slow down. It sounds so cliché these days, but this is when you truly need to stop internally, take an inventory of everything you have, and express gratitude. Simple but effective. And we're old enough to remember the slogan for Virginia Slim's cigarettes that became the catchphrase for the women's rights movement: "You've come a long way, baby!"

Yes, you have. Not only appreciate what you have but how far you've made it. Your evolution is just beginning. Like I said at the very start here, you're still learning. Hopefully, one or two of the words I share here will resonate with you. Or, if this book is just sitting on your coffee table and you haven't read a word, at least your puppy dog Sparky may be getting something out of it when he chews it up.

Aftermaths produce so much that's different. If the concept of acknowledging signs is somewhat new to you, you could be more comfortable with the notion of calling them experiences. Repeat experiences. They happen, just as they always have, but after your life-changing event and aftermath, you'll know that these experiences are happening for a reason. They're directly related to your purpose, and they're meant to happen, so you'll learn.

Did you begin to recognize some repeat experiences after your own life-changing event? Consider the following examples:

- You missed the same offramp for the second, third, or fourth time because you were going too fast, focused on speed, not destination. (Lesson: patience.)
- Every time there's a job opening at your employer, you pass because of "bad timing" or some other poor excuse. You find that you're not considered the next time because you have passed so many times before. (Lesson: appreciate opportunities that are presented to you, there's never a "perfect" time for anything.)

Aftermaths are also great at exposing patterns, some that should have been killed off long ago. It goes without saying that the bulk of life patterns that existed before your life-changing event need to be destroyed after your life has changed forever. You'll create new ones that more directly align with your true purpose.

If you discover you have lung cancer, it'll benefit you to stop smoking; you'll appreciate you and your life more. Life's difficult enough; obstacles are thrown our way all the time. Some are lessons, some are not. So much is out of our control. But one thing we can control is how we take care of ourselves. To stop and reflect on our own needs is vital; it's also a part of why we're here in the first place. Mother Teresa wouldn't have become a saint had she not cared for herself properly throughout her life. She lived to be eighty-seven. You first, then martyrdom. Great work, if you can get it.

There's no question that the period following your life-changing event is the most potent time of your life. It's also where you become more cognizant of time and timing. It's not perfect timing because, like we said, there is no such thing. That notion keeps us so far from our goals. When looking back to my own pre-life-changing event, I didn't recognize or appreciate "surrender" at all. It was always full steam ahead; I never seemed to allow myself to put anything on the back burner. Do you control time and the experiences contained therein?

The aftermath of your life-changing event not only brings your purpose (your lessons) into sharp focus, but it also matches you with your passion, your truest and most unobstructed desires. You may have several. It's never too late to begin again. Your aftermath empowers you when recognized; it lines you up with a path to achieve your goals and solve problems. All because you are now living your true purpose, as you also see the lessons you were meant to learn. It's time.

It could even be a "Whew!" moment. A sigh of relief. What was yours like? Your immediate aftermath? You can get on with the rest of your life, *or* you can begin your life. It's revelatory. I felt this way, and I was so grateful to discover the truth that existed in my life, a mystery solved. This necessary discovery prolonged my life. Have you discovered yours?

As you continue to read, reflect on your own reality. Consider how it's changed. Reflect on those challenging times you used to tolerate that you now accept as "lessons you were meant to learn."

You have my sympathy if you're still living with trauma. I don't know if it comforts you, but it's the best I can share: *everyone* suffers. Makes you feel less alone. Makes you feel for others and what they're going through. I mentioned a few times earlier that learning compassion for others is a lesson for me, but in these times, perhaps it's more universal than I once thought. Yep, for sure. Are you a compassionate being? If so, were you born this way? Or did you learn compassion over time?

After feeling like the mystery of my life was solved at the end of 1991, it didn't take long for reality to sink in. Harsh reality. Protective mode came upon me, big time. Oddly, understandably, as I began to mature emotionally, my shell grew as well.

Discard my example completely if you cannot relate. In the long run, my discovery of the truth led me to live longer, be free, and be independent. My wish is that you discover yours if you haven't already.

Living Free

This is something for you to think about at present. How free do you feel right now? Are you still reliant upon anyone for your own happiness? Survival? Wellbeing? I don't know your circumstances, but I surely respect what you're able to change and what you cannot. Most situations are extremely complicated. I seem to have met several folks who appear tied to their spouses because of joint financial commitments when they'd probably be much better off if independent. I've never been married, so I can't speak on divorce court, but when I think of the word "protection" used there, I cringe. Marriage? Eek. Better be sure of what you're getting into so your freedom's not compromised. Think long and hard about the word "love." As far as I know, and not to be flippant, there's no magic wand attached to its spell.

Retirement doesn't guarantee freedom, either. Attaining financial freedom later in life means you've earned it. You made that happen. Kudos to you. For others who fear their future financial outlook, continue to save and, more than all else, know the value of money. Retire when the time is right, and don't jump the gun. Be prudent as you age so you can keep "lack of money" fears at bay. Did you know that less than 1 percent of Americans retire before most want? Sixty-nine percent of U.S. workers plan on retiring by 66, and 89 percent of the same are not fully retired until 75.[5] Best to mentally and fiscally prep now.

How much alone time do you offer yourself? Even if you have a lot of responsibilities in your life, giving yourself alone time is far from selfish. Don't wait 'til you take a vacation to schedule it. Time to yourself, especially time spent in nature, should always be allotted in your calendar. It's where the answers come to *you*. Again, aftermaths yield the big picture. They put things into perspective. No matter what your lessons may be, life-changing events and their aftermaths help you recognize a force much greater than just yourself.

Wisdom comes *after* life-changing events, disasters natural and unnatural. In the fall of 1989 (prior to my life-changing event), I had been living in that downtown San Francisco apartment I'd mentioned earlier, where, as you may later on deduce, I ended up living for thirteen years. I wasn't really a baseball fan, but I just had to turn on the TV that afternoon to watch the baseball World Series. A rare occasion, because both participating teams were within the San Francisco Bay Area, the Oakland Athletics and the San Francisco Giants. I propped myself up in my waterbed, a can of Tab in one hand and the remote control in the other. Play ball!

After only a few minutes, my apartment on the twenty-first floor began to shake violently. A massive earthquake measuring 6.9 on the Richter scale. Enormous damage. No water, no power, no electricity. Everyone in my building was focused on survival. We all exited the stairway and dispersed, not knowing if we'd have a place to live after we left the building. Unaware of where to go, I followed others—me and strangers—to the closest place where there were no tall buildings we'd believed would crumble above us. Levi Strauss Plaza is an open and secure area. I positioned myself next to a woman who had been listening to a portable radio. "The Bay Bridge collapsed!" she yelled out. Panic was everywhere. Looking towards the bay, I saw the bridge and noticed no damage. Dark was approaching, and I chose to leave the area to walk to the top of nearby Telegraph Hill. The vista there displayed a war zone. All of San Francisco with no lights on, many fires blazing, and nothing but sirens to be heard.

Certainly, as a senior individual, you've experienced a similar catastrophe within your lifetime. Do your best now to recall a fear that had consumed you, how you lived through it, and how your life forever changed from moving beyond it.

When you're in fear-induced survival mode, you don't have the luxury of thinking bigger picture. There's no time to wonder *why* this was happening. If it was meant to be or not. Like others, I was just aiming to make my way through it.

In the fall of 2001, nearly a decade after my life-changing event, I experienced another life-alterer. Again, at my beloved

Lake Tahoe, I turned on my computer first thing in the morning and logged into AOL. The front page displayed a dramatic image I thought was an ad for a disaster movie. It was 9/11, the attack on the World Trade Center. Though I was geographically far from the tragedy, terror invaded the lives of many folks around me because so much was unknown. I called a friend in the Bay Area, and we talked about it. "I hear they're going to blow up the Golden Gate Bridge next," she'd said. Panic, shock, and fear rippled through me.

Who knew what to believe? Like everyone else, I was in self-survival mode but sought something larger than the fear that was right in front of us all. I got myself cleaned up and chose to go outside for a walk through the forest and then along the shore of the lake. I began my walk by asking God a question before saying thanks. Sounds crazy. But to some—maybe more than some—the notion that the world was coming to an end was a real possibility. Nobody really knew what was to come next.

I honestly don't recall my question, but I'll never forget what came to mind most strongly, what I felt right then at that moment. Appreciation. I was thankful for being at Lake Tahoe. Grateful for having been there so many times, the place that's like my own (outdoor) church. The place that's most like Heaven without having to be there. I said something like, "If the world's to end soon, I'm so grateful to be here." Fear left me. It was replaced by something greater, something so much more comforting. In a rather abstract way, it was the first time I felt unafraid of dying (by any circumstances).

My literal aftermath of 9/11 was nonexistent compared to those who were impacted by this tragedy. *Anyone* would feel compassion for them. And, I did.

Discovery of my own truth, my own life-changing event and its aftermath, led me to my true purpose: to feel for all others (no matter what). We graduate from "juvenile" to emotionally mature thinking once we choose to learn our lessons. Do the work, and you won't be sorry.

Compassion ain't achieved overnight. It all begins with forgiveness. Lessons come from circumstances, events, and signs, but inevitably, some of the most significant ones come from our own parents.

Looking ahead, seeing, and understanding the bigger picture, will help you *tremendously*. It will help you accept that maybe you don't understand much. Much of what's out there cannot be explained away. And the folks in life who are seeking apologies or expecting the other person to change are, sad to say, delusional. Do your best to see the good because there truly *is* good in everyone. *Everyone!* And always be grateful in equal measure—for having been given life *and* the lessons attached to it.

Forgiveness *Is* Divine

Have you forgiven everyone you felt has wronged you? Anyone? Have you been selective in your list? There's always going to be someone, something, or some situation that doesn't match up to what you deserve or what you feel you deserve. The older I get, the more imperfect I realize *I* am. How about you? The more imperfect you realize you are, the easier it will be for you to let others off the hook. Voilà! No matter how much you feel you were wronged, you're forgiving yourself when you forgive others. When you're a mature adult, the "But I didn't do anything wrong!" defense is no longer valid. It's a child's answer.

According to Karl Pillemer, a Cornell University gerontologist, for folks aged seventy to eighty, their number two regret of their life looking back is not having resolved a family estrangement.[6]

There are so many, but here are a couple of examples of forgiving others = forgiving ourselves:
- You hold it against a friend for reneging on giving you that job they'd promised you. Years pass, you let it go, and you (figuratively) forgive that friend while at the same time admitting you didn't deserve that gift and felt unqualified for it in the first place. It's not their responsibility to make you believe in yourself; only *you* can do that. (Lesson: You get what you deserve; appreciate any offer, accept only what you're worth).
- You keep running away from people, places, and things you feel don't suit your needs. You enjoy where you are to the best of your ability but perpetually feel there is better over…there somewhere. You never become a part of any community because you're never anywhere longer than a few months or so. We must stop blaming the who, where, and what of it all and instead appreciate the variety life has to offer. We must forgive all previous blame and accept that happiness only stems from within. We must forgive ourselves for continuously hunting for it elsewhere. (Lesson: You are all you need to make yourself _____. Anything beyond that is gravy.)

Right now, forgive yourself if you've ever beat yourself up because you didn't know your purpose. Now, you do. Take a load off if you haven't already. Take in a very deep breath, knowing that your purpose has been with you all along. You were born with it. No more searching for it with a flashlight after the power goes out. It's with you in the dark and in the light. Less overwhelming, ain't it?

Learning lessons and living your true purpose doesn't take money, education, qualifications, or cable TV; everyone receives their lessons equally. Everyone's got a purpose, and it's up to the recipient to own up to the fact that they've got something to learn (in this life). It's up to them to be taught or not.

Slow and steady wins the race. A cliché? You betcha. But it's true. If you aim to learn all at once, you won't be here. You'll be in that pine box before it loses that mountainy scent. Kind of like a freshly mopped floor doused with Pinesol. You'll never have to stagger your lessons to fit all into your busy schedule because that's already done for you. Another cliché or adage or whatever, but you are never given more than you can handle. True. No adjustments to your calendar are necessary.

And, when you get a break, make sure to enjoy the downtime. Lessons will always be there, but those breathers arrive few and far between. When you take a break, when it comes your way, or whenever you feel you've earned one, enjoy it to the fullest. It's like a Hawaiian vacation minus the sandfleas and tar. Once you choose to learn a lesson of any size, a sense of accomplishment will overtake you, and you'll know that a break is headed your way. It's like confirmation that you "did the right thing" by having chosen to learn this time around. No repeat lessons. Well, not for the moment, anyway.

Breaks are like residing in Heaven's "holding pattern," a unique place and time where lessons are nonexistent. We only do those here on Earth. Heaven must be like a massive vacation. No traumas, no heavy loads, no counting WeightWatchers points. Heaven is a rest stop without those filthy toilets. A beautiful, serene, unhurried retreat where no definition for the word "lesson" exists. But, on the other hand, it's the place where you're rewarded for having chosen to learn.

Are you pissed right now? No, not drunk (British English). Are you angry because someone has the gall to say that you've gotta be dead before you'll be rewarded? Hell, no. You would have cut my ass off at Chapter 1 had I said this. Trust me when I tell you, when you choose to learn a lesson—any of the many lessons you were born with—you're gonna feel a sense of accomplishment that's unmatched. Unlike any feeling you've ever had. Applaud yourself for having earned that raise, for having put Jimmy and Joanie through college, for buying that house. They're great accomplishments, but they can't come close to why you were purposely relocated from Heaven to Earth.

You're here for a reason. You're here to learn lessons. This *is* your purpose in life. Period. This *is* what you're here to accomplish. Exhale big time once you accept this as a fact. You're big boys and girls by now. If you're reflecting on legacy-building at this point in life, this is it! Lessons learned. Mission accomplished. Thank you, sir. May I have another? Only time will tell, but more than likely, you will. Lucky bastard.

Life here means different things to different people. A place with a finite formula. A place where work, love, vacation, advancement, suffering, triumph, and more are all seen as separate or combined numerators, a bevy of lessons, the common denominator. Everything else ÷ lessons = why you're here. A mathematical equation that even Joey Tribbiani and Rose Nylund can understand. No finger or toe-counting for the solution. Chrissy Snow may still need to go to summer school for this, but the rest of us? No. Moving on.

Mid-terms and Final Exams

Hey, you've earned another *A+* just for hanging in there with me. Thanks. If I haven't said it already, it's the smartest people who ask the most questions. So, let's proceed from where we left off. Shall we?

Lessons aside, what made you choose the life you've

created for yourself? Question your why. Was it out of desire? Necessity? A little of both? To go with the grain? Because that's what's done? Think about it because the time's come to compare and contrast.

Like most of us, you've probably believed your purpose in life had to do with _____ (fill in the blank with anything but "learning lessons.") You're not alone. When I used to pencil in, I ended up wearing out my eraser every time. <u>Acting.</u> <u>Entertaining.</u> <u>Writing.</u> My answer kept changing before I had my life-changing event. Yes, it's that pivotal. Early on, all those years, I had confused purpose with desire. I should have taken the time to better differentiate the two. What did I want most? To be <u>validated.</u> Hard to make a living at that, but it's extremely common for survivors of trauma or narcissists or children of narcissists. To be seen, valued, acknowledged.

My aftermath gave me the wisdom to know the difference. Lessons learned along the way made me see a human being in the mirror, not a human doing. I did not need to be an actor, an entertainer, or a writer. I didn't need to be *doing* anything to feel worthy of any kind of life I was living. Have you ever thought about that concept? Human being vs. human doing? Buddhism refers to this as "attachment." It means identifying ourselves based on what, who, and where we're attached. Human *beings* need no attachment. We're good enough as is. We've been so conditioned to accept that what we do, choose to do, and are destined to do is our purpose in this life.

Only in recent years do I see a winner in the mirror. What do you see when you look in yours? My hope is that you find a victor in your own reflection. You'll be glad you did. I already told you at the very beginning of Chapter 1 that you're a winner. What more do you need?! Once more, compare and contrast the life you've manufactured vs. the stuff that keeps seeping through the cracks of it (your lessons, your true purpose). Great if you see value in both because there is. One doesn't exist without the other.

Why did you choose to live your life the way you have? Why did you choose this specific path? I told you before that those "why" questions are the hardest. You agree? Much more thought-provoking than the standard yes-nos. I've always believed that it's at this stage in life, the mature side, retirement or near retirement, when we are most ripe for the "whys." This is when, more than ever before, we need to know most definitely why we are here. What's the point (of it all)? Why did I do things this way or that?

Again, makes me reflect on those folks in Silicon Valley the most. Those folks in their 50s, 60s, and 70s on the 24Hour Fitness treadmill in Cupertino who've programmed their workouts for 30:00 on the dot, not a second less, not a second longer before moving onto the free weights. Precisely in between their global conference call and business lunch. All within their master plan. I'm not being critical; I admire them tremendously. All believe in themselves and their goals to no end. Oh, how I envy both.

But then the time on the treadmill hits 30:01, the cool down. Maybe on a day prior to retirement. Maybe when their kids leave for college. Maybe when their spouse files for divorce. A fulfilling, accomplished life that took blood, sweat, and tears to actualize. Praiseworthy, maybe even enviable, by all accounts. But, now what? Think of yourself being on that treadmill right now. The timer just turned 29:59. What's going through your mind? Ask yourself, "Now that I've accomplished (just about) all I set out to do…or not, what's left?" This represents a huge moment in our senior lives.

What happens next? And what does it all mean? Why am I here? What's my true purpose? Wow, that's a lot of questions. Before turning to drink, pick just one. And since it's just one, make it a "why" word question.

The timing couldn't be more perfect. If you've focused almost exclusively on accomplishing tangibles all these years, now, as a retiree, your life may be just beginning. No one ever said that tangibles are more valuable than intangibles. If you haven't yet come up with your life-changing event, maybe this is it, all because you—indirectly or directly—asked for it. Like I did. My life-changing event was instigated by my "why." "Why can't I have a relationship?" Eek! Be careful what you ask for. And, be sitting down when you get your answer. Your life will never be the same again. This is a good thing.

Change is good. Retirement doesn't mean your productive years are behind you. You're just recalibrating them. Time to jump back on that treadmill, now with a different focus and no agenda. Simply ask "why" the moment you step on and see what happens.

Lessons are a full-time job. They're not trivial, not for killing time, and should be taken seriously because, let's face it, who wants to see their ass every minute of every day? Best to tackle lessons head-on so they appear in intervals, sort of like commercials when ad-free viewing is not an option.

Everything's digestible if taken in small doses. Just look at those ~~fools~~ folks on *Survivor*. It doesn't necessarily take courage to swallow lessons, but it does take a willingness to acknowledge they exist in the first place. It's much easier when you concede that they've been in your life from the start. They weren't put there by accident. You must be daring and courageous to tackle any lesson, but when you experience the masterful sense of accomplishment once you've graduated, you'll be ready to conquer the next.

TAKE ACTION

Now you know that you're still in school, please write or dictate your answers. Take as much time as you need. Looking at the aftermath of your life-changing event from then to the present may require you to cover a lot of territory.

- *Do you feel you have matured emotionally since? If so, how?*
- *Have you matured as a direct result of your life-changing event?*
- *Are you wiser now than you were before? How so?*
- *More than likely, you've learned several lessons along the way; do you (now) feel you're living your true purpose?*

Pencils down.

4

TRUTH

As in your work life, you create success by building it one step at a time. So far, you have re-defined what "life purpose" is. You ask "Why?" a bit more frequently. You've gone back to identify exactly when your life purpose was thrown in your face, a time when your life-changing event defined the beginning of the "new you." Its aftermath reignited your purpose, and now you're living it.

Next, you'll learn the ultimate might of living truthfully by accepting no substitute. When you ask why now, you'll never question the veracity of its answers. Nothing is more authentic than truth. You'll be made aware of its multitude of benefits and feel the depth it adds to your life. Here, you'll learn to see and feel deception instantaneously. When you live only the truth, you deserve nothing less in return. At the end of this chapter, you'll be asked to measure how much truth you're currently living, pushing you to live your true purpose completely.

*F*ocus on yourself, and everything else will fall into place.

Live the truth, and your life will be your own. How many

times have you tried to change someone? When did you learn that you can't? Trying to change anything about anyone is not only a lose-lose situation, but it eats up your life and your life's purpose. You're here to live *your* life, learn *your* own life's lessons, and create changes within yourself. A win-win when learned. And while you're at it, steer clear of pretense, exaggeration, and little white lies. They seem more harmless than out-and-out lies, don't they? Wrong. Equally perilous. Just as inauthentic. Instead, be brave, be an open book, and your pages will be filled with freedom.

It's all on you and begins with acceptance, even if it means accepting the truth unconditionally. Only you can live the truth; you cannot force someone to live theirs. It's their thing. So are family secrets. There's no need for you to keep secrets of any kind; it will inhibit your own growth and prolong old, already-existing lessons you're ready to tackle and eliminate right now.

Have you ever noticed how much better you sleep at night when you keep no secrets? When you have no untruths stored up? A perk to being a sociopath, I'd imagine. They can sleep through anything! (If you're not already being honest with yourself) the truth will set you free. Fibs make life a bit easier, but only in the moment. You still have to live with them, and they definitely do add up. You grow so wise when having the courage to live the truth; you're learning lessons when surrounded by the truth. And it goes without saying that there are huge consequences to perpetuating lies. They are self-serving and take you far away from selflessness and compassion for others.

Again, we're not responsible for others or what they're all about, but sometimes, it's easy to see what lies can do to people.

Have you seen evidence of lies equaling consequences? Within your own life? In the lives of others? We see it on the news all the time, but all we need to do is look into the mirror to identify their proximity to us and the lives we lead. Their aftereffects may not be immediate but still linger and destroy. Deadly. As dangerous as fear itself.

Some say that fear is the devil's energy. Something that no one would want. If fear's in your life, it's not there by choice. Whether you learned it, were born with it, or feel you deserve it, living the truth combats it. One step at a time, lies keep us stuck in fear. Sometimes, taking that leap into faith just isn't possible when fear becomes so ingrained. Even if you're not religious or spiritual, the word "faith" is great even when used solely in the abstract. Apply it to yourself and see what happens. If faith can move mountains, you certainly can, as well. BYOB. ~~Bring~~ Be Your Own Bulldozer.

As seniors, we not only have more wisdom but a much greater assortment of tools at our disposal to make our lives easier. They're there for the taking. Use 'em or lose 'em. If truth's not in your supply kit now, add it!

Truth in a Nutshell

Many definitions exist for truth, but for you, there is only one. It's quite personal. But, in the bigger picture, it's universal. The same positive attributes are out there for all to reap.

- In and of itself, it's mighty. There's infinite power in living and speaking the truth.
- Keeping a lie alive or living with one is the most harmful toxin that exists.
- Exposing a falsehood you've been keeping—or one that was told to you—is emancipating and leads to your sovereignty.
- A lie that you know about that was created and kept by others is *their* karma. It's their problem, not yours to solve.

- If someone is controlling you or another with a lie, they're perpetuating a false narrative. Do not accept it as your own.
- If it's a lie you told or had to live with, rectify it. There's never a perfect time for anything; replace your lie with the truth right now.
- Living the truth initiates a spiritual life, where everything you recognize in your life is either meant to be or not. It's easier to accept everything once you do so.
- There's no going back, but take one moment to reflect on moments in your life when you could have told the truth but didn't.
- If you haven't yet, challenge yourself right now to think of one truth that you've been too afraid to accept. Even in the abstract, you may see in the distance how easier life will become overall once you set yourself free.

Coming Out

In 1980, singer Diana Ross had another hit single, "I'm Coming Out." Where were you when it was released? I recall first having heard that song as I exited the Berkeley BART (Bay Area Rapid Transit) station while on my way to school. We all know this chart-topper. Ms. Ross has had many, but this one had special significance to the gay community. Diana Ross was unaware, though. She "didn't understand" that "I'm Coming Out" could be considered "a gay thing." Pardon my use of so many quotation marks. If you're old enough to remember, there was a time when gay people weren't called gay but were known as "different," "special," and "fancy." Times have changed, and it's comforting to know that adjectives (different, special, fancy) have been replaced by nouns (gay, LGBTQ+).

"I'm Coming Out" has a broader meaning these days. What does it mean to you? Maybe you're coming out of retirement to live your purpose and learn your lessons at this very moment. It can be an anthem for anyone who chooses to live freely, truthfully, without inhibition. Leaving a lie behind could be a lesson for a lot of folks living with a variety of circumstances these days. Living a secret, false life is passe, though we must respect everyone and the "restrictions" they see and feel. Living authentically often depends on how much pain a person can tolerate by living falsely.

From the beginning, I've primarily seen the word "gay" as a noun, not as a verb or adjective. Born that way. I remember when I was twenty-one and had just moved to San Francisco. I lived in the financial district (the Silicon Valley of the 70s and 80s), which was very proper. A new friend of mine said, "You need to go to the Castro."

The bulk of the population in that part of the city was gay. Many, many transplants there. Although the area appealed to me, I didn't feel compelled to spend the majority of my time there just because there were so many gay people. I didn't feel duty-bound to fit in. It didn't take me a long time to "come out," and it was quite uneventful. I happened to be gay, had a variety of all kinds of friends, and was never discriminated against. I lived truthfully then and still do. Many years later, after my departure from San Francisco, another friend asked, "You're moving to *Lake Tahoe*?! Who are you going to meet there?!" He was alluding to the fact that it was not a city, not San Francisco, full of nature lovers. "I don't care who I meet or don't. I love that place, and that's why I'm moving there." I'm grateful to be comfortable with myself wherever. I hope you feel the same; feel free to be yourself.

Truth lives in your actions as well. What you do, what you rely on in order to make it through. Pay attention to what you hear and what you see, especially to those things you keep recalling. They could be big or small. They may not even resonate at the time. Perhaps you're not ready for that, but when they come back to you, they're coming back for a reason. They're meant to.

Example: I had a friend I met at the gym at Lake Tahoe in or around 2001. Thomas was extremely personable. He came off as light-hearted, but there was depth inside him. The gym is where most folks chitchat, but he tolerated me and my perpetual "why" questions. I knew he was a recovering alcoholic, and he was very committed to sobriety. One day, I questioned him about this by asking, "Why did you quit drinking?"

"When you're in an altered state, how can you see what God has in store for you?" I don't recall exactly if he used the word lesson or not, but it didn't take much for me to grasp the significance of Thomas's answer. Common sense, yes, but profound at the same time. He was so correct. When we are in chaos, when our minds are altered by alcohol and drugs, when we're surrounded by toxic people, we cannot see lessons as lessons. We may not be able to see much at all; we're entwined in life's dramas without learning from any of them.

I didn't get it so much at the time, but I look back to that one comment made by Thomas, and I'm still awed by what he taught me. I always saw this one statement as truth, although I wasn't ready to live it until several years later. Addictions are so very common in our world; they're everywhere. Watching celebrity reality shows can be addictive, but when we're getting off by viewing their tirades and tantrums, something wrong is going on with us. We become as noxious as they are. I am just as guilty. Remember *The Anna Nicole Show*? I used to love that one. I used to love gossiping as well. Even more unhealthy. If you've got a grandmother who told you, "If you don't have anything nice to say, don't say anything at all," trust her because she was right.

Vice Versa

A recent study co-authored by University of Wisconsin professor Tony Docan-Morgan indicates that most people are honest, telling only zero to two lies every day. In the study group, lying made up 7 percent of all communications, and nearly 90 percent of all lies were little white ones.[7] Congrats if you're "most people."

If you're not already living the truth, know one thing for certain: if you're brave enough to live and speak honestly all the time, you deserve nothing less back. You don't deserve lies, and you don't deserve to have your integrity questioned. Nothing is more offensive than the latter. If you're friends with someone, and they know you well enough to know that you're an honest person, living the truth, beware when they question you. Look at your friendships right now. Appreciate those who value the truth. Appreciate those who value you and re-evaluate your friendship with them if you find they don't value you fully.

Your life-changing event is the biggest event happening in your life. Period. Think of what it would be like if a friend of yours questioned the existence of it. I had a friend for many years who was quite loyal and helped me out on several occasions, and I feel I did the same. I still think highly of her even though we are no longer friends. At a time when I still talked about the discovery of my past, the discovery of my childhood, my friend would ask, "So, they admitted it, your parents? You have evidence that this really happened?" My friend asked me this on several occasions. I can accept these questions from a stranger but not from a trusted friend.

Trust needs to be earned, and friendship only occurs when trust is reciprocal. If you're doing your work (learning your lessons) and your friend, any friend, is not, your connection becomes too imbalanced. Not just trust, but mostly all values must be in sync. And, if you're a giving person, never be in a friendship where your friend wants you in their life to learn their lessons for them. It doesn't work that way. You do your work; they do theirs. We weren't put here to learn others' lessons. Beware of friends who show up out of nowhere and want something from you.

Friends from the past are in the past for a reason. Social media keeps you stuck, whether you realize it or not, to people, places, and things from the past. Life's lessons are progressive. One leads to the next, leads to another, and so on. They become different in type and seem to be more advanced as you make your way further in life. The more you've learned, the more complexity you can tackle. Let's be very clear, though; it's not those friends, it's you! God bless those friends; they're to be appreciated for who they are, where they are, and what they're about. They're learning lessons at their pace…or not. They are not you. Lesson: Be open to new, and only accept what you deserve right here, right now.

Your aim is to graduate, to learn, to move on, and to master the lessons you were born with. Living truthfully helps tremendously by not keeping your lessons camouflaged. When you live, speak, and exist only in the truth, your lessons are going to be inescapable. Ready or not, here you come. You and your lessons become one. They are you, and you are them. Nothing gets your life unstuck like choosing to learn a lesson. Bam! The ball's in motion and doesn't stop until it hits a wall you put up. Just like Ronald Reagan once said, "Mr. Gorbachev, tear down this wall!" He did, and the rest is history. Seeking peace and unity is one of the all-time great lessons!

Just as lessons repeat for a reason, so do the words I throw your way. My objective for you remains the same: to help you inspire yourself one step at a time. As a senior or not, if you struggle with everyone else's concept of success, achievement, and fulfillment, it's time to replace "theirs" with "yours." By this point, you've made the effort to re-define the meaning of life's purpose. You've identified your life-changing event. You've absorbed—or continue to absorb—its impact. Congratulations! You've come this far; how about taking another step? No, we're not playing Twister, and although life may appear similar to a board game, it wasn't created by Parker Brothers.

  Go ahead and pass go and never choose the same piece when you start over. Variety gets you unstuck as much as living the truth. Sometimes, the truth needs discovering. When I exposed mine, my life genuinely began. Most narcissists would never ever admit they are one, but when I realized I was, it smacked me in the face. Thank goodness it didn't leave a mark. My reveal came from my questions, all one million and one of them. How about you? How much of your own life do you question? Do you question even more now that you're retired? Having a less cluttered calendar should allow you the gift of time to both question and answer.

  If you haven't realized that you're responsible for everything that happens to you in life, now's the best time to do so. Don't even bother questioning others because you'll never get the correct answers. Those answers are not available to you, nor should they be. No overtime is given for solving others' problems. So, to be most specific, at this very moment, question your life and the truths (you believe) you live with. Are some "facts" masquerading as truths when they're really lies? Step back and observe your own life as an outsider would.

  You've already questioned your life purpose. Now it's time for more. And don't take the easy route out—begin every question with why. Note the following examples:
- Why do I feel unworthy?

- Why am I afraid of retirement?
- Why do I seek validation from others?
- Why do I feel compelled to have a full calendar?
- Why does being alone terrify me?

Each answer will expose a truth, I guarantee. Each question, the deeper it is, will take more time to ponder. Each will lead you to expose your true purpose. Once you know what that is, the more fulfilled you will feel. You're doing what you were put here to do: learn your lessons. Yours. Again, focus on yourself, and all will fall into place. Whether you're an over-giver or pleaser (and expect answers or not), they always come from within. From your intuition, most likely. Whether you were conditioned to call it "female intuition," make the correction now. All genders have it. All humans have it. Maybe all animals, too—I'll have to ask Sparky.

Look back right now. Look at your life objectively. With no emotion attached. Rationally. Which obstacle keeps recurring? Which problem never really disappears? My "why" questions led to my life-changing event. Do yours? Pop your life-changing event, your turning point, your bottom, back into your head for a bit. Identify without hesitation the most significant crossroads you have ever faced. All that's left after you do that = the truth, the whole truth, and nothing but the truth.

Now, the rest is up to you. You've got to live with yourself. I got to a point where I couldn't had I not discovered and accepted my own truth. Ultimately, an answer exists for all questions. Your answer. The one that makes sense to you. It doesn't matter if others don't understand. And be very discerning when others question you. They've got their own agenda going on, or they may be too afraid to face their own truths. Do you know of folks like this? Are they in your life? Were they? Above all else, whomever they may be, know where they're coming from.

A few years ago, a friend from my past resurfaced. She was cordial on the surface when she wasn't handing out backhanded compliments. "Gee, you don't look as fat as you used to." Not everyone knows how to be sensitive or diplomatic, but when you see a pattern of these types of remarks coming from the same person, you can be sure their criticisms are intended to put you down. If you choose to keep friends that offer these disguised insults, that's for you to ponder. When you realize you deserve better, you have learned a great lesson. There's better out there, I promise. And, if you don't find these new friends, you're still left with the best there is: you.

Boundaries are great but don't forget, when you put up a wall around someone you already know, remove it when you meet someone new. New acquaintances and friends don't deserve those same barriers, if any. Know what you deserve and accept nothing less. New folks are not coming in with the same agenda(s). It's also extremely difficult or impossible to change or reconfigure heretofore-established friendships when you're living your new and improved you. If you've been a giver or pleaser, some old friends will still take and expect that you'll give. I don't think they can change this. Instead, thank them for who they are and what they meant to you, and wish them nothing but the best. Wish (for them) that they learn lessons freely and easily. And move on.

When your number is called at the deli, race up to the counter. Even if you're vegan or a vegetarian, dine on the meal you've been longing for. It tastes even better the longer your mouth waters. Don't drool, though. It's a bad look. And while you're at it, steer clear of gimmicks and trends. They're manufactured and marketed to the masses for a reason: a quick and easy sale. Be—and live—your own trend!

Are you a sports fan? Have a favorite athlete? I've been a longtime athletic supporter. The most consistent interests I have in my life are tennis and tennis players. Fifty years and counting. Over the decades, I have always favored the number two ranked player vs. the number one. Number two, Arantxa Sanchez-Vicario, over Steffi Graf. Number two, Andre Agassi, above number one, Pete Sampras, and more recently, between 2005 and 2010 or so, number two, Rafael Nadal, over number one, Roger Federer. There's something about the person who's both high-ranking and underdog at the same time that captures my interest. They're at the top but still have something to prove. Most people are enamored with number ones. If you're old enough, seniors are like Avis; we try harder. Sorry, Hertz.

When reflecting on your own life and how yours compares to others, though, there's no need to measure. Leave the leaderboards to the pros. If there's someone you aim to be, let them inspire you. Learn from them. Remember the lesson I told you about? Getting over myself. Having compassion for others as a result. Being content wherever I happen to find myself. Having said this, here are some questions for you:

- Why have I lived this life?
- What led me to live this way?
- Was my life predestined? Or did I create it myself?

For that last yes/no, please explain. Gives you something to think about, doesn't it? While you're thinking, know that you're not alone. Never. With seven billion or so folks on Earth, there's gotta be more than a few who share the same thoughts, feelings, choices, decisions, and destinies as yourself.

If you think your truth is unshared, wait just a second. No truth is unique.

Very shortly after I had my life-changing event, I ran into someone I knew, a woman from the tennis club where I had worked. Her name was Marilyn, and our chance meeting delivered big time.

Marilyn asked how I was (after a bit of small talk) and offered a seemingly genuine, "What's new?"

"It's so strange. I just had this very weird experience. May I tell you?" Her nod gave me permission. "I know you're a therapist...I just found out that my parents were into devil worship."

She said, "Oh, my," or something similar. I don't really recall how she reacted, but she didn't exhibit alarm.

"My father's partner raped me. They were on the Oakland police force. My father shot him, killed him." How I said this with no fear, I also don't remember. But it was Marilyn's calm I remember most. I'm grateful to her for that. There was a pause that was supposed to be there.

"When did this happen?" she asked.

"The early 60s."

Marilyn nodded like she knew. "Clint, that's who I treat. In Marin. A clinic up there, patients."

"Who?"

"This happened here during that time. In the Bay Area. Victims of Satanic Ritual Abuse. The early 60s. This happened to you?"

"Yes. You help them?"

She nodded yes. "But, you're the only person I've ever seen who's not institutionalized because of it. You can still function."

I looked back at Marilyn with awe. For me to blurt out what scared me so much and for her to allow me to do so and respond with care and concern, I will always be grateful. In that conversation, the clue that sounded like horror fiction was indeed real. I even learned others live with that same reality, that same truth. We are never alone.

I hope so much that there's a Marilyn in your life.

Someone who's an outsider and shares no allegiance with you but comforts you in a familial way. A person who offers you an unspoken subtext that says, "Everything's going to be alright." I hope you have this. I hope you had this. Sometimes, folks on the outside, even strangers, provide the finest exchanges. Surprise conversations while out on a walk are what I like best. Maybe my expectations and standards are too high when talking to folks I know. I usually despise small talk, but when talking to a stranger, it's not realistic to expect otherwise. As a result, you're never disappointed. Be open to new connections, even if they last only a few minutes. You'll make each other feel good, I promise.

In the meantime, appreciate truths. It's not person-specific, either. Facts are facts. Just as my body and mind hurt and grieved as a child, my family must have as well. It took me many years to see our shared mental and emotional states. When too busy dwelling on me, I branched out. I opened up slowly and saw that this was not just my truth; it was theirs, ours.

How do you view your family? Now that you're a well-established adult, do you view your parents differently than you used to? What did you learn from them?

How many times have you heard, "Never point out your weaknesses?" It's oftentimes advice given to folks launching new businesses and entrepreneurs following formulas devised by others. It depends on the business. If you want to be relatable to most, be human, be vulnerable, and let it show. How can we possibly learn from others if it's difficult to relate to them? I think life was meant to be simple. A simple and succinct plan is given to all: live and learn. A three-word dictum for our 50, 60, 70, 80, 90 years of existence.

An advantage to aging is that telling a lie becomes more difficult the older we become. According to a study conducted by Brandeis University, published in the *Brain and Cognition* journal, adults over 70 may lack the cognitive know-how to compellingly tell a lie and recall the made-up facts later.[8]

Dumbing Down Works

If your mind leans towards challenging and advanced thoughts too often, choose to go simple for part of your day. Where I'm living now, there is no cable TV reception, and I subscribe to no streaming services. There happens to be a DVD player, though, and every morning, I pop in a disk from my box set. *Mama's Family*. The full six seasons of silliness revolve around a Midwestern family commanded by an acid-tongued matron. Her son and daughter-in-law live in the basement, and her grandson's out on parole. Thirty consecutive minutes of mindlessness that fosters a smile every time. What's your guilty pleasure?

Mama's Family is not just a simple American sitcom from the 80s. It depicts authentically unadorned lives, lives that are real. And that's why the show's funny to me. It's real and simple, with a bit of absurdity thrown in for laughs. Much of life is absurd. Or that's how many choose to see it.

How do you see your life? Any absurdity in it? Does any of the real make you laugh? I hope so. Joan Rivers taught us to laugh at ourselves. Do you? As a kid—every week—I couldn't wait to see Mrs. Drysdale show up on *The Beverly Hillbillies*. Remember her? Wearing those expensive outfits, furs, and such. Her body unable to exhale from those tight-fitting costumes. Too funny. Someone pretending to be something other than what they are, not being able to relate to those hillbillies, and despising them for not fitting in. How gauche!

Maybe there's a bit of pretense in all of us, though. A pinch of Diane Chambers, a smidgin of Mrs. Drysdale, and a speck of that snooty neighbor that moved next door to Roseanne. You know, the one that makes that needle-butt sneeze. It takes a lot of effort to be something you're not, to pretend, and if you're aiming to be a comedian, truth is (most definitely) funnier than fiction.

Speaking and living only the truth yields big results. It declutters your brain, for one thing. "If you tell the truth, you don't have to have a good memory," Judge Judy says. Hey, since we're all getting older, the timing's perfect for this. We'll all be more truthful because of physiology: diminished capacity. How convenient.

The truth is funny. Change is funny. And, yes, looking back is funny. Personally, I look back to all those years I didn't like myself so much, all that self-imposed exaggeration. I never thought embellishment was lying until I looked back at my LinkedIn profile. Yes, I did study German, French, Spanish, and Italian. I did live in those countries and attempted to speak those native languages to the best of my ability, but was I *fluent*? Fluent in all four? Are you kidding me? Not even close.

Do you ever exaggerate? Inflate your attributes, accomplishments, or skill levels just to impress or jump the line? Come on, fess up. It's funny to look back when you appreciate honesty above all else. If you like who you are, don't exaggerate. There's no need to be pretentious. Pretense is filler. Truth is the real you. As we become older, being the real you is not only good enough; it's what's most fascinating to others.

Try a little of that today. Expose something real. No, don't be a flasher! There's still a time and a place. Try being as honest as you can be in a single day. See it, live it, and show it. With yourself and with others. Within reason, though. Never give T.M.I. Don't force anyone to cringe.

On a serious note, gotta repeat, and this is an obvious one, a biggie: When you're honest, speaking and living the truth, insisting on it within yourself, you'll be able to recognize untruths (in others) immediately! In a scam-crazy world, you'll be susceptible to fewer than the average person. You won't be taken in as frequently. Doesn't promise that you'll always get the same truth back that you've dished out, but wouldn't it be great to better spot inauthenticity with no second-guessing?!

Let's bring up instinct once more. It's quite similar to truth-telling/living. It's right 100 percent of the time, and it's the most underutilized asset we possess. It was given as a gift, so it is best to use and appreciate it before the sender asks for it back. Accept all your instinct tells you, and when you're listening to it, don't try to make sense of it during the moment. Just put your rational mind on mute for a few seconds. Never question it, even though you will anyway. Agree to take it all in courageously. Bonus: A great way to stave off the static for a time as well, an instantaneous respite.

Your authentic purpose will become obvious. No longer the dolled-up version. Ken and Barbie belong in your childhood box of belongings, not behind your steering wheel. And, just as Phoebe Buffay pointed out, "What's up with Ken's 'smooth' area?" I agree. In the gym locker room, I've never seen any guy with one of those.

If you're still wondering, let's go cliché. The truth *does* set you free (and then some). It liberates you and the life you live like you'll never know. Start now and let go of any "what ifs" and "if only's" you have lingering around. If only *Mama's Family* matriarch, Thelma Harper, would have known in advance that she bought a bum blender from RayMart. What if she'd actually won the Grandma USA pageant and didn't come in second? Or had changed places with that snooty Cousin Lydia? The truth of the matter is that we all make mistakes. Not every one of us is going to win a beauty pageant, and comparing our life to anyone else's serves no purpose.

Sitcom characters aside, be grateful for what you have. Seeking the truth within yourself and the life you've got surrounding you is going to leave you feeling more enriched than you can imagine. Use whatever adjective you like: blessed, endowed, lucky, glad. There are so many. The one that pays the most dividends is grateful. Always wanting more or what you feel you don't have takes up a lot of space inside your diary. Try shaving a few items off your to-do list and see if you even notice a difference.

Productivity is now relegated to AI. If we continue to measure our worth based on how productive we feel obliged to be within a day, we're sunk. All of what we *do* is being replaced. Our life's purpose is what we learn from it, and it will *never* be replaced by AI. AI is 100 percent outside ourselves. Be satisfied with yourself and your own RI (Real Intelligence).

TAKE ACTION
Ask yourself and divulge (by writing or dictating):
- *What's my story? What was my truth growing up?*
- *What's my truth now? Am I living it fully?*
- *Is there someone or some situation that—I feel—prevents me from living my truth fully?*

Be honest.
- *In what ways specifically could I be living more truthfully?*

Ask yourself:

"What now?"

5

REPEATS

The past repeats itself if you don't learn from it. Here, you'll be asked to notice repeat lessons and hopefully acknowledge their significance so they'll vanish for good. Lessons only serve you when learned. Early in this chapter, you'll see how some lessons are finite, specific to certain individuals, and how some exist for millions at a time. Focus on yourself, but be aware that learning lessons is reciprocal, an equal-opportunity teaching.

In this part of the book, you'll see how retirement could be the best time of your life: your chance to "do it all over" and assign the most value in your life to the part that was not planned out but given to you. You'll question the choices you've made prior to retirement and ponder what you may now do differently. You'll value time more and integrate free time without feeling guilty. You'll be asked to list many of the repeat lessons that have come your way. You'll be urged to master them and add to the pride you feel for having done so.

To be successful in the here and now, you need to be fully in the present. The past is in the past for a reason, but it becomes quite dangerous if you haven't learned from it. What did you learn about life when you were a child? Anything? Oftentimes, a little lesson learned lasts a lifetime. If the recognition of pain begins early, why can't its remedy? Go back to that time. What made things better? Before you ponder, be proud of how far you've come.

So far, you've re-defined the term "life's purpose" for both yourself and in the broader sense. Once that's been established, your foundation's been set. By identifying your most important/prominent life-changing event, you jumpstarted the way you see and experience the life you're living in the deepest yet most obvious way. You re-examined the immediate and sustained aftermath of your life-changer and acknowledged the lessons that were once hidden from you. You now recognize the extreme power of living the truth, expressing it while no longer settling for the acceptance of anything less. You only deserve what's honorable. It's more challenging to live life this way, but the rewards are never-ending.

You've mastered two of the most crucial questions life poses: "Why am I here?" and "What's my purpose?" Great if you've answered fully or perfectly fine if your answers are works in progress. You're doin' it. It's only natural that next you turn to, "What now?" because there's a ton.

What have you learned as an adult that stems from a lesson introduced in childhood? Have you experienced any of them more than once? How often do they repeat? What have you learned from your personal history that's become a part of you today?

Insert Yourself Here

Because we're of a similar age, fellow retirees, see yourself in this universal ~~story~~ lesson I'm about to share. Where were you during the Civil Rights and Free Speech Movements?

The Vietnam War and its aftermath? The turmoil and unrest of the countercultural 1960s? Let's take a trip together.

As a kid, I learned my best history lessons listening to a car radio for hours at a time driving north on Highway 101 while sitting in the passenger seat. It was the mid-to-late 1960s. My mother and I were living in Playa del Rey, a suburb of Los Angeles, and I attended St. Anastasia Catholic School in nearby Westchester. I was only eight at the time of the Watts rebellion (also known as the Watts riots; if you don't know this, Google and learn). The Civil Rights movement was everywhere, but I don't necessarily remember discussing it in school. I don't remember my mother and I talking about it either, but when you're sitting in a car for a seven-hour ride, there's no escaping the news in between Beach Boys tunes.

My mother—now divorced—regularly drove us to the East Bay in northern California for family visits. These trips went on for a few years until we ended up moving back. This is where a lot of learning took place—inside the car. In those three or four years, I noticed that things were changing in a big way. I didn't understand everything that was going on; I just knew it was all something significant. Riots, protests, and such were taking place everywhere. On one of these visits, my maternal grandfather, Sam(uele), an Italian immigrant who was able to avoid Mussolini's imminent draft as a youngster, took me flounder fishing. We'd done this a few times in the Bay Area, but on this occasion, he was taking me to the Berkeley Pier. "But Grandpa. Berkeley? That's where they kill people!" I hadn't known that the pier was independent of the University of California campus where the Free Speech Movement—and protests against the war in Vietnam—were taking place.

I don't recall if either one of us caught any fish that day, but I kept learning. I certainly didn't know it was a lesson at the time. A mighty lesson for all. As a kid, I took it for granted that when things change, they change for the better. Well, that's not the way it goes. As a kid, I thought, due to the vast education I'd received via the car radio, life's lessons = a done deal for us all. White and black people can now get along fine because we're all equal. No more to fuss about. And then, on a car drive north, live on the radio, I'd heard that Martin Luther King, Jr. had been shot and killed. Why? But...a done deal!?! Apparently, the shooter hadn't caught wind that we're all supposed to get along now.

I learned so much from that car radio, but I never could explain why. *"Do You Know the Way to San José?"* was played often on KHJ, and it always used to make me smile, mainly because we always used to drive through it. My smile stopped when the next song came on, "Abraham, Martin & John," a sad one. In my young mind, I thought Dr. King died so we'd all know, once and for all, that we're all the same. That's what it took.

As we all know, it did not take. Racism wasn't eradicated in 1968, after all. Nearly six decades later, we've still got a long way to go. Pardon the pun, but lessons don't adhere to our well-delineated black-and-white terms. They repeat. Lessons repeat. History repeats until...well, you know the rest. I look back, and I'm grateful. At such an impressionable age, I got to absorb what I was witnessing: the Civil Rights Movement, the Feminist Movement, and the Gay Liberation Movement. I learned from all three. Huge steps forward. I never thought I'd see gay marriage exist in my lifetime; appreciate your rights while they last.

As seniors, the pace slows. Every year after age 30, you lose about one heartbeat per minute off your maximum achievable heartrate. That's 40 less if you're 70. This deficit decreases blood flow and circulation.[9] Not wasting it becomes paramount. Do you agree? The signs are everywhere, aren't they? Recognizing lessons when they recur adds time to lifetimes. Some lessons remain mysteries, but you're already more than familiar with the vast majority you'll experience. No surprises at all when they decide to make a comeback. Not at all like any Met Gala, lessons show up year to year wearing the same identical gown as before.

Lessons don't exist on a stopwatch and don't care how quickly you learn them. There are no prizes given for speed. They're content to last as long as prescribed; there's no expiration date printed on the label. Repeat lessons show up in life as experiences, situations, and occurrences from which we learn, and they never appear as a coincidence. Many times, they yield positive surprises.

Example #1: You've just finished your weekly grocery shopping and haven't paid attention to the lengthy lines up front. Yikes! All have three to four folks waiting, mostly all with carts filled to the brim. As usual, you're in a hurry. Not only did this become an opportunity to practice patience, but it also yielded the chance to re-think your needs. Maybe there's an item or two you'd forgotten to pick up in your haste. You leave the line and choose to travel through the store, finding the few extra items you realize you needed in the first place. When you return to the checkout area, you discover that there are only one to two people waiting in line. (Your lesson is patience.)

Many times, lessons show up as twofers. There's a double whammy going on; you think it's one but realize it's two or more things. These twofers present a golden opportunity for multitasking your way through your life's purpose. Extra credit when you're able to identify both lessons right off the bat, recognize they are repeats, and are assured that this time, you're going to get it right.

Example #2: You walk into the tanning salon you've been going to for a while. A simple, quick, and easy twelve minutes a week that gives you some color and makes you feel good. No one is at the desk to greet you, and when someone arrives, it's not the friendly young girl you're used to seeing; it's the owner. He is an abundantly macho guy who never looks you in the eye when he speaks. He never says hello, but you do.

"Hi. My last name is Smith."

The owner says nothing.

"Tony," you say.

"Sorry," he says.

"Tony."

"Sorry."

"You're sorry my name's Tony?"

"Just being funny."

"Not funny. It's bullying."

The owner cannot believe you finally called him on it. He had done this twice before, but you laughed it off. Not this time. Kinda scary at first, confronting a guy twice your size. You didn't expect that this would leave him at a loss for words, and your gut tells you that you're there to get a tan. It's not that complicated, not worth creating a scene, and you did what you did not do last time: spoke your truth. You did it without bullying back; you didn't need to. If Michelle Obama elects to go high, so can you. You did something good, positive, and wildly productive. You overcame fear to demonstrate how you deserve to be treated, and you remained kind to the man you'd once been afraid of. (Your lessons are speaking up for yourself and having compassion.)

Still referring to this example, when you notice it's the owner and not the amiable young girl you're used to chatting with, don't freak out. Encountering him, not her, is not an annoyance, a nuisance, or an obstacle. Something so good comes from it when you see it (as early as possible) as an opportunity for learning and growth. For your own and for your teacher (the tanning salon owner) as well. It was no coincidence that he tried pulling something on you a third time. It was meant to be because you didn't choose to call him out prior. A mutual lesson to be learned.

Life provides us with repeats for a very valid reason. There's also no hierarchy when you've got several to learn. On any given day, you could be given a lesson having to do with patience, another having to do with being more compassionate, and out of nowhere, one unrelated that you've never encountered before. Still a lesson, of no greater or lesser enormity, the same value as any other.

Example #3: You enter the always-crowded grocery store perfectly calm. You're in no hurry. You shop patiently and find everything you're looking for. You've forgotten nothing, and when you go to check out, you find that no one is standing before one particular line. There are still a couple of items on the belt, though. As you load your items behind those, a man pushes his way past you to get up to the cashier. He adds an extra item he must have forgotten. It's the tanning salon owner. You realize it's him, and he recognizes you. "Sorry," he says, followed by, "Hi." A half-smile comes after that. He wasn't a dick because of what you'd taught him about having been one. He now treats you with the respect you deserve. He may push other people around and offer no kindness while doing it, but no longer to you. You learned a lesson, and so did he (in relation to you). A joint venture. (Your lesson is assuming others stay the same, never change or grow.)

Lessons work both ways. Where people are involved, there's a teacher and a student. And sometimes vice versa, involving the very same lesson. Also, once they're tackled, they're not repeated. You're more than likely never going to see that tanning salon owner again. No more to learn or teach.

Here and Now

Pack your bags. You're about to go on an adventure. Instead of grabbing your Samsonite from the luggage carousel, you're going to take your lessons. That's it. Nothing more. On the outside, you're wearing your comfy clothes, but on the inside, nothing but your birthday suit. Hope it still fits. This is all you need when going from past to present. At this point in life, you've accumulated a lot, so try your best not to forget a thing. Once you pack, there's no going back.

The present is a great place to go. The past taught you a ton, but it's grown rather stale, hasn't it? Kind of gone downhill. Run down a bit. Just like The Jeffersons, you're movin' on up. To the East Side, the West, or somewhere in between. No need to tip the doorman, though; slip that Hamilton into the palm of your own hand instead. You've earned it.

Because lessons repeat, so do the chances, the opportunities, to "get it right," to do better this time. A noticeable improvement from the last. By now, you've re-defined the meaning of your life's purpose, you've identified your life-changing event and its significance in your life, you're fully aware of its aftermath, and you're living your life truthfully. You've never been better prepared to enjoy the here and now of life, to appreciate repeat lessons. What fun we're having! Right?

Remember, without lessons, you wouldn't be here. So, be grateful for them. They are badass. So are you. Another thing to recollect: lessons are always given to you. It's never the other way around. They're given to you whether you want them or not. But, to play fair, there's one thing you control. Yes, learning those lessons. You do control that. But, when a repeat lesson arrives at your doorstep, there's something new you can do about it: a do-over. Remember those doers perpetually climbing those StairMasters (or whatever they're now called) in Cupertino, Silicon Valley? Well, now you and they are one. You're all doers, and you all have the chance for do-overs.

Do-overs! Huge! Second, third, and fourth chances to hit your mark. Another venture to capture that one that got away. And do you know why you want to do it right this time? Because you never want to see that $#%$#% lesson again. Let's face it; it's a pain in the ass to begin with. Who needs it?!? After the fourth, fifth, or sixth time, all you want to say is, "Good riddance!" Best to appreciate it for what it is, but after that amount of time, it no longer suits you. So, when you get your chance, muster all the courage that's inside you and embrace your do-over!

Hey, that looks familiar! Well, of course it does. It's the lesson you let pass by yesterday. It's another chance, another opportunity with similar circumstances yet presented at a different time of day. One that—when it's recognized for what it is—is just waiting to be learned. Waiting for you. An unintended entry that's put in your calendar at the very last minute. When these lessons repeat—opportunities that have come around again are not recognized for what they truly are—you may see them as nuisances and say, "Sh—, are you kidding me?! Not this again." Oh, yes. A lesson. Duh. Have you ever said this? Questioned repeats? You're not alone.

Is learning patience one of your repeat lessons? Seeking validation? It doesn't matter whether you're validated by anyone. When you're patient, you validate yourself, and that's all that's necessary. People don't get to you because you're more focused on yourself, doing what you intended to do in the first place. If chaos ensues, so be it. That's life. So much of the world we live in (with others) cannot be controlled. Best to be patient with all. Start saying, "More lessons to remind me, please."

Many profound and insightful quotes regarding life lessons usually have something to do with "There are no do-overs in life" or something similar. In several respects, this is true. You can't undo the past; you can't undo anything that has already happened. But, with relation to learning the specific repeat lessons that come your way, *yes*, definitely. You can most certainly do (the lesson) over and change its outcome. Ever heard of continuing education? If at first you don't learn, try, try again.

Recurrent lessons coming to you may not match the ways in which they were delivered previously, but the lessons themselves remain the same. Like a friend asking for your financial help when you have little to give, yet you give anyway. Soon after, your dishwasher floods your kitchen, leaving you with a mountain of repair bills. Years later, you're doing fine financially, yet that same friend lets the restaurant tab sit on the table, expecting you to pay it. They're also doing fine. Why should you pay all of it? A lesson that came back. Did you learn from it the first time? Second? Third? After you've learned your worth, you no longer accommodate and please. You've learned your lesson. Keep it that way.

If learning to be happy or feeling worthy of happiness is a lesson of yours, you're ahead of the game. A study by the *Journal of Clinical Psychiatry* found that older people are significantly happier than younger people.[10]

So many rewards exist for choosing to tackle a lesson the second, third, or fourth time around. The lesson may be the same, but its severity changes the more you learn from it. They disappear quicker, too. No doubt that they're going to return, but their duration may be short-lived once you know you're up for the challenge of absorbing them. One thing that prolongs the duration of any individual lesson is how you react to it. If you react with impatience, irrationality, chaos, or confrontation, all that attention and energy is missing the point, the reason for the lesson in the first place. For some, learning to respond without reacting is a lesson in itself.

Don't whine! Whining doesn't make lessons disappear. It helps in no way at all. Be glad when lessons re-arrive. How very lucky you are that a lesson comes back. Sometimes, it takes reflection and time away from the lesson the first time you encounter it. You responded the way you did, and the lesson still comes back. This means one thing: you didn't learn the lesson or didn't learn it fully.

Fact or Fiction?

Once upon a time, there lived a person who many felt had everything. Purposeful Pat. Pat, about to turn 65 in a few weeks, ate, lived, and breathed everything tech. Pat was a master at seeing trends lightyears before they materialized. Pat lived in a ten-thousand-square-foot house in the Saratoga, California foothills and worked as an executive at a prominent social media company in Silicon Valley. Pat's kids, a son and a daughter, adults now, moved out of the country after seeking out more balanced lives. They were not as driven as Pat; they had no desire to put ambition and achievement above all else. Pat made sure to succeed in all areas of life, not merely in the career world alone.

Pat had made sure Jamie and Geoffrey had the best of everything: private education and master's degrees from Stanford and USC, respectively. Any parent would be proud. Family vacations to Europe and beyond created memories to last forever. Jamie and Geoffrey both began families of their own and, via heritage, sought out dual citizenship in Italy. They'd both told Pat that they happened to learn the exact same thing once they first arrived in Italy. To be understood most precisely, Jamie, not so fluent in Italian, heard in English, "You Americans live to work, Italians work to live." It took a bit to sink in, but Jamie began to recognize this as being the truth, not just an Italian's take on

Americans.

Geoffrey, already fluent in Italian, didn't need any extra time; he saw this adage as truth immediately. This is when he initiated the citizenship process. He saw much more to life than what he was witnessing in Silicon Valley. Though Pat had two grown kids who moved and created families far from their nest, over-achiever Pat still felt balanced in life. Pat valued traits that were common in Silicon Valley: achievement, excellence, and teamwork. Laudable, for sure. Pat felt that a commitment to a career, all those years keeping a steadfast plan, would propel anyone past any obstacle.

Pat, newly separated and now empty nester, was still attached to one of the most recognized names in social media. As a well-respected top executive with nearly two decades of seniority, Pat was an influencer with clout. Pat was thought of as a guru and would oftentimes speak at economic summits and events, inspiring other engineers, computer specialists, and programmers. Something to be proud of.

Just when divorce proceedings were about to commence, Pat received news: termination before planned retirement. A surprise twist no one in Pat's circle saw coming. Pat, who benefited from meditation, regular exercise, a good diet, and a moderate amount of self-care, felt overwhelmed for the first time by questions that were brand new and not obvious. All Pat had thought about previously was being able to remain financially secure, retaining and managing as many assets as possible without compromising personal and professional security. For the first time, Pat had to accept that not everything can be controlled in life. Pat questioned control. Who has it? Why did this happen now?

Those questions got the ball rolling in the most unobvious way. After about a year and a half after the divorce became final,

Pat had a revelation or two. When looking back, Pat had realized that a life-changing moment had taken place, and its aftermath had now become the present. The truth hit Pat square in the face, and it was time to face it with no filter. A year and a half later, Pat was ready to master the toughies that were entered into Google Calendar a year prior:

- Why did I live this life?
- Did I buy a Tesla merely because everyone else did?
- My kids are gone and aren't coming back. Where do I go (now)?
- I provided all and more for my family. What have I given to myself?
- What do I call myself if I'm no longer a CIO?
- Why am I here (in the first place)?
- What's my purpose if I can no longer be productive?
- What now?
- What's next?

Somehow, Pat took a deeper dive than just dipping both feet into the pond. Pat, at first, thought that doing something very different and fulfilling would fill this new void. Creative writing had always been a goal, way before the foray into technology, the practical and productive route that came about through paternal and maternal influences. Not Pat's first choice by a longshot. Family won out, the family Pat was born into and the one that came after. Choosing to be a novelist at 65 was merely one ingredient of something so much greater than making a career change later in life. For the first time, Pat did something Pat wanted to do; Pat made a decision solely influenced by Pat and no one else.

Now, 66 and a half, Pat knows that that life-changing event didn't lead to a makeover but a do-over. Not doing something differently, a different and new way, but much greater: a lesson

Pat recognized from adolescence, "Put myself first, be happy in my own company, no need to please others at all. Even if writing creates no success, it still is because I am doing it entirely for myself, and I don't care what others think of this decision."

Now a well-established senior citizen, Pat is fully independent and chooses nature over nurture. A contentedness surrounds Pat. Spending mornings writing with no expectation, walks in the Sierra Nevada mountains alone but not. No family, no coworkers, no friends or pets needed. After that life-changing event or a series of events all added together, Pat needs no title. No caption. Now that Pat is self-sufficient in every way imaginable, anyone who enters Pat's life is gravy, not the main ingredient.

Such a fast learner. Pat went from a life-changing event at 65 to learning lifetimes since. Pat's do-over is anyone's do-over. They are offered to all. Some come by surprise, and others are manifested by desire, but all should be appreciated. They're all gifts to become unstuck and live life with authentic purpose. With all the questions Pat had been coming up with prior, a friend had asked Pat after the fact, "Don't you miss it? Your old life?"

"Yes, I guess I do. It led to meaning."

"Meaning? What kind of meaning?"

"Without all that, my past, without appreciating it all, my wonderful family, my work, the way it panned out, I wouldn't have landed here."

"So, you're cool with all that?"

"Hey, I'm about to turn 67, and I wouldn't have it any other way. So grateful for every second of it. More bonuses now than when I was working."

Maybe the super-ambitious are the ones who learn lessons at lightning speed. Good for them. Good for Pat. Some of us on the journey of life bring luggage bought from Kohl's only after redeeming our Kohl's Rewards points, while others carry around Louis Vuitton. Maybe Pat changed retailers after life changed, maybe not. Doesn't matter. Any person's lessons are their own, but Pat is neutral for a reason. There's a bit of Pat in all of us. I think Pat is a fascinating person. I'm not exactly sure what a CIO does, but that's what Internet searches are for.

Do-overs and Don't-overs

There are things you do and things you don't. DO your best and DON'T expect. Nothing's more dangerous to anyone than expectations, especially when you expect another person to change just because you did. Don't expect anyone else to see things the way you do; they have their own points of view and perspectives and view life from a lens you don't possess.

As a child or adult, have you ever thought about running away? Well, in 2004, I intended to do *everything* over. I left my old life, became a European citizen, and never intended to come back to the United States. Without admitting it at the time, I was running away from my past. And it sounds crazy, but it kind of worked until my past came back to haunt me.

After several years of living in Tuscany, Copenhagen, and Munich, I felt a calling to return to the U.S. for a do-over with my father. It was 2006, and I hadn't spoken to—or seen—him in thirteen years. I thought I never would again. I had always expected and demanded an apology from him. That was my *huge* mistake. Time to forgive.

We got together near his home in the Las Vegas area, shared a few meals, he drove me around, and we interacted with the wild mules at Red Rock Canyon. A wonderful memory. I loved it. This experience was a do-over of grand proportion.

Forgiving. A byproduct of my purpose in life: learning

compassion, a common lesson for millions. There *is* good in everyone, especially inside my father. It wasn't until much later that I cultivated compassion for him and accepted him for all he is vs. what he did. Maybe he *was* protecting me after all. We never did become best friends following that visit. After my return to San Francisco, I called him on his birthday. It was pleasant enough. A few months passed after that, and when my fiftieth birthday approached later that fall, I wanted (not expected) a card or call. Didn't get one. My lesson #2: Stop giving. Lesson #3: Stop seeking validation. Lessons learned.

Somehow, I see all lessons as being reciprocal. There's always a teacher and always a student: it works both ways. I wonder if I taught my father anything. Secretly, I felt that he admired the courage and determination it took me to discover, deal with the truth of it all (the murder, the abuse), and confront it head-on. One more time, there's power in truth. The most power.

The way I saw my three days with my father was like taking an eraser—to all the guilt I'd presumed he'd had—to a chalkboard. I washed it all away, but I was sadly mistaken about thinking I'd made things right. In mid-2011, Father's Day was approaching, and I was living in London. I sent my father a card and mentioned that I'd call him in a few weeks. I called, and his most current wife answered. Never had a problem with her. Cordial enough. No small talk, though.

"Didn't you get my email? Your father died six months ago."

The truth: best to expect it with no sugar coating.

There's another word that's just as powerful as truth, though. You probably already know what it is: acceptance. Accept things as they are. Accept the truth as you know it, and don't expect others to live by that same truth. You never know what's going on inside their minds. And never expect friends, strangers, or anything in between to understand you. When they tell you, "Just get over it," it's because this is all they know. They've presumably not done their own work. They remain an unhealed work in progress and deserve understanding. Move on and be proud of yourself for tackling the lessons on your plate one at a time. Accept friends and family for who they are and be open to making new.

Timing is Everything

Lessons are always available to us, but we do control the pace at which we attempt to learn them. So, pace yourself. Strategize if you can. I had an exact goal in mind when meeting with my father: I wanted to clean the slate. I wanted to clean his and clean mine at the same time. If you're wiser than I, you'll know that you cannot do this for another person. Cleaning the slate is *your* lesson (for you), not anyone else's.

For you, the same. Lessons are quite often delivered with triggers. You already know what yours are. As retirees, we're mature members of society, and our agendas are not as full as they used to be. Thank goodness for this. You've got moments thrown into your day to let things sit before needing to respond (while never reacting). You have no say when repeats are delivered to your doorstep, but you certainly decide when picking up that package, taking it inside, and opening it. Those last three steps are your prep, your planning. The do-over begins once you make use of its contents.

In addition to having fewer allergies and infections because of having warded off colds, the flu, and infections through the years, senior immune systems have good memories. Allow more outdoor freedoms. What a luxury age is; all that wisdom you've collected, all previous lessons learned or not. Your call.

Take a nap, power or otherwise, in between lessons, and chances become great that you're gonna nail it, big time. When you're a senior, no credit is given for putting out fires. Learning lessons creates preventative medicine. As far as lessons are concerned, putting out fires equals fanning the flames. It's all drama, reaction to chaos, frivolous. Stick to substance, and you won't be sorry. Do it over when you're good and ready (best prepared, having learned well from the last lesson, and remembering how you could have done it better). Now's your chance. Take it.

Take it Easy

After taking chances and taking action, it's now time to take it easy—something do-ers have difficulty with. Whether you're a fan of the Eagles or not, loosen your load. Glenn Frey must have had seniors in mind when he wrote, "Lighten up while you still can." Along with maturity, retirement is a privilege. Wisdom is severance pay that mounts up and never terminates. Before investing it into your next lesson, though, count your blessings. If your blessings = the wisdom you've accrued, you're in great shape. If not, keep counting. Everyone was born with buried treasure inside them; you just gotta use the right tools to do the digging.

TAKE ACTION: Part 1
As always, you've got the option to write or dictate. If you choose to type, please print out when done.
- *List all the repeat lessons that have come your way, all you can think of. They don't need to be listed chronologically; random is just fine.*
- *List as many as you can think of, and don't dispose of this*

- *list or audio file.*
- *When you're done compiling and printing, post this list in front of you somewhere.*
  If it's an audio file, re-play it every once in a while, when you need to refresh your memory.
- *Mix in lessons learned along with your repeats; they're the most valuable things you own!*

Bon voyage!

TAKE ACTION: Part 2
- *Refer to your list of repeat lessons to be learned. Which ones returned that you chose to do over? There could be many.*
- *Do you feel you were successful in learning them?*
- *For those you feel you've tackled, afterward, did these lessons start to appear less frequently within your life? Did they disappear altogether?*
- *Keep adding. Try entering only the ways in which you'll tackle those lessons that are directly attributed to your purpose.*

The more you master them, the easier your life will be to understand; you'll never again need to ask why you're here or why certain things happen to you (over and over).

6

~~PERFECTIONISM~~

You've come so far. Re-defined the meaning of the term "life purpose" for the collective and specifically for yourself. You've identified your life-changing moment, the clear-cut emergence of your real-life purpose, and the power and truth that aftermaths bring. You're busy rectifying repeat lessons, and now you stop for a bit by surrendering to what's perhaps meant to be. In this chapter, you'll be guided to rest, relax, and live your life independently, away from the sway of others.

You'll find that signs and synchronicities appear when they're supposed to. You'll see here that mistakes are your teachers. They inevitably lead you to what you deserve vs. what you don't. In this chapter, you'll be encouraged to schedule alone time into your calendar or add it spontaneously. More than all else, you'll be aided in getting unstuck by doing something different on a daily basis and being thankful for the gradual changes it creates. You'll see worth in living the simple life vs. keeping up with others and what they are doing.

*I*f you think you're hard on yourself, you're not alone. In today's world, perfectionism is imposed on us all the time—to be new, improved, and better than our old selves while keeping up with the Joneses (the Kardashians of yesteryear). That's a lot of pressure and expectation. Whether you're from Silicon Valley or Southwest Bronx, fuhgeddaboudit.

You've done some great work, some deep digging. Now, you deserve a break. Here's where you step back and observe just how much is being done for you. You know that expression, "Help is on the way!" Well, it's already here and has always been. This is the time of your progression that you don't need to gauge or measure how far you've come. You're here right now, in the moment, and that's when you've earned the right to just be and reveal all you've learned. Mathematically, what's done behind the scenes totals more than anything we could ever do on our own.

We'll talk more about the dividends surrender provides later on, but for the time being, we're discussing its antonym, perfectionism (aka control). You can only do so much, and when you know you can't do anymore, let it be. It's like applying for a job. You want it, and let it be known you want it. You submit your resume, you may follow up, and you want to appear like the perfect candidate, yet what may interest the interviewer most is one of your *im*perfections. But you hadn't planned it that way. Because you're not perfect. Instead of trying to figure it out, be grateful for that unplanned, unexpected, and uncontrolled moment. That imperfection could be the quality that gets you hired.

I never did watch *The Simple Life* when it was on, but I'm pretty sure Paris Hilton and Nicole Richie were on to something. Back to basics and unadorned while still looking hot. Well, sort of. It doesn't take much…to be happy. A walk in the park. Time spent petting your cat. Seeing your grandchild smile. A pleasant conversation with a stranger. There are tons and tons of things that generate contentedness once you let go. Control, expectation, unrealistically high standards, and perfectionism all bring us further away from the thing we seek most. These are all qualities we can change.

Forgiveness is divine, and we feel it immediately when we give it to ourselves. No one likes making mistakes, but let's get real: they happen, they've always happened, and they will continue to do so. We're human. I wonder if any of the other animals beat themselves up for drinking regular coffee when they know they should be drinking decaf. Maybe that's what makes squirrels so jittery.

Instead of beating yourself up for making a mistake, celebrate when you don't. Celebrate your flexibility. Your ability to not be in control all the time. You know why? Because it ain't gonna happen. Life doesn't work that way. You may think you'll be able to attain perfectionism when you're younger, but when counting the years that are left, nothing shaves them off your calendar more quickly. It's harmful to never be satisfied with what is. Makes you sick. No vitamin supplement remedies perfectionism. The best prescription is to let go of control and abandon busyness. Allow wiggle room for the unknown. Appreciate that white space in your calendar; it's just as valuable as anything entered and saved. It's unknown for a reason. It will undoubtedly be filled in with something out of your own making.

Are you a planner? Do you create your day on the fly? Or is there already a good deal of balance within your DNA? Take it from me. Spontaneity was never my thing. My old friend Randy and I used to watch *The Golden Girls* together. He'd say, "You are so Dorothy!" I scowled; he knew how much I wanted to be Blanche. Dorothy: Practical. Me: Prone to propriety; it's like we're twins. That was the 80s. Which Golden Girl were you? Which one are you now? Best answer: a bit of all four. In our world today, malleability runs the show. It's impossible to live stress-free without it. Perpetual migraines if you don't.

The same goes for perfectionism. Your version of perfect is subjective; it's the way you view it. You've got to be open every once in a while: open to a more perfect plan, a more perfect purpose that you may not be open to receiving right now. You were born with this perfect plan; it includes the lessons you were given at birth, those perfect ones that make you wanna scream into a paper bag, then crumple it up and burn it in the fireplace. Not nearly as good as s'mores over a campfire, but close. Yum.

The compulsion to be busy also needs a bit of tweaking. Busyness? What is that exactly? I think the best things happen after quiet contemplation, maybe in nature. You're rewarded many times over, more closely connected to your purpose, and you move along, achieving at a pace that extends your life.

Also, train your brain to be optimistic. It's never too late. In a study published in *Proceedings of the National Academy of Sciences (PNAS)*, people with higher levels of optimism lived longer. Results of those surveyed found that 50 percent to 70 percent of optimistic men and women possess a greater chance of living to 85 than those least optimistic.[11]

Signs and Synchronicities

When you need it most, there it is. Your recognition of signs and synchronicities goes far beyond being a perfectionist or not being one. It's sort of related to your own instinct, the most powerful tool you possess, but it's more like an offshoot. Synchronicities are those helpers that arrive seemingly out of nowhere when big decisions need to be made. A friend who confides in you that she's about to start therapy right when you've been thinking of doing it yourself. Two people not knowing what the other is doing or about to do, and yet they are in sync: a blatant sign. Blatant if you believe in such things, a "coincidence" if you don't.

Just like people, coincidences and signs love to be appreciated. You'll get more when you do. I mentioned earlier that you're gonna hear some things, see some things, or experience some things that you're going to remember forever. Think of those right now. What's the most significant? Which one ended up being memorable that you'd initially felt was insignificant at the time?

Like my friend Thomas (at the gym at Lake Tahoe) explaining why he doesn't drink. Well, I had another biggie while living there having to do with creative writing. My wish was to complete my first novel and do it perfectly. You guessed it. There *is* no perfectly.

While at my desk, finally disciplined enough to write daily, I somehow couldn't compose another word. Never good enough, I thought. This was in the year 2000, and I happened to have the *Donny & Marie* talk show on in the background. Donny happened to be discussing the pressures he'd felt all his life to be the best, all the time, to please people, to entertain them.

The intense need he felt to be perfect for himself, his fans, his father, and his family debilitated him. He admitted that he was diagnosed with social anxiety disorder and suffered from panic attacks.

Donny talked about the moment when he recognized that *trying* to do his absolute best was indeed good enough. He realized that there is no such thing as perfect. He seemed to show everyone that doing your best is not only all you can do; it's always the healthiest option.

That story came in when I needed it most. What story came to you when you needed to hear it most? Did it stick with you 'til this day?

In your own life, if you look hard enough, you'll more than likely notice signs and synchronicities every day. They could be all over the place. Whether you need them or not, they're out there. You'll most often see them as mini-validations of what you already know. You may be thinking of taking some sort of action. You already know what it is. Let's say you've chosen to start a business by catering seafood snacks, lobster on a stick, and finger food. Something rather different, specialized, so you wonder if there is going to be a market for such a thing, but you proceed without knowing for sure. You conduct minimal market research, but your gut gives you the go-ahead. Just at the time when your bills are really piling up, doubt enters your mind. Again, your gut is telling you, "¡Vamos! (Let's go!)" This is when your rational mind needs to be silenced, just for a bit. It talks too much as it is.

You've done as much prep for your new business as possible; it's as perfect as it's ever going to be before you seek out clients. You're at the wharf, scoping out the catch of the day. Ideas are popping into your head having to do with new and innovative ways to steam cod and sell it as a tasty and healthy alternative to fish and chips. As you stand at the dock waiting your turn, two younger women, chatting feverishly, approach you rather impatiently. "How long have you been waiting?" they ask.

"Not long."

Are they talking about waiting in line at the fish counter? Or how long you've been thinking about launching your fish-catering business? A hidden and camouflaged double entendre? Who knows. The two women not so silently discuss their dilemma of putting together a last-minute beachside luncheon for their fish-eating AA sponsor. One thing leads to another, and…you've got your first clients.

There's only one here and now, isn't there? I'm not so

sure, but I've been told that there's no time like it. The present. Did Dorothy ever appreciate being in Oz while there? She certainly did learn a ton from her journey, but all that attention was spent on returning to Kansas. Really? Well, her journey, not mine.

Again, when reflecting on SVS (Silicon Valley Syndrome), I tended to see folks who were perpetually in the future. No conversations were needed; their faces told all. Their ambitious nature was impressive, but the "having it all" mentality was hard to relate to. Europe was my home from 2004-2011, and all the belongings I'd had to my name fit into one suitcase. That's it. Nothing more needed.

When you're content to carry only one bag with you, you're not bogged down with nostalgia, and you're not obsessed with creating more. You're complete and completely satisfied as is. You've redefined the word perfect. Perfect = as is. On the other hand, when the back of your mind operates on a having-it-all framework, it overrides the present. Nothing takes you out of the present and into the future more than perfectionism, the notion that you must have it all.

As mentioned earlier, timing is everything, but perfect timing is not. You know why, right? Again, that notion is imaginary. It doesn't exist. Waiting for the perfect time to do, to act, to say something is nuts. It takes you completely out of the present because you've transported yourself into the future. Leave all that to the characters on *Star Trek*.

Look back to your younger self, the one that kept waiting and waiting and waiting, making up excuses, feeling that you needed to be perfect in order to do X. Let that person go. The older you looks the way you look. More than looks, though, wisdom is the one asset that counts most. And it always ages well. Very well. You know why? Because we weren't born with it. You cannot inherit it, and it's impossible to bribe your way into getting it. The one and only way to acquire wisdom is to earn it. It's your reward for living your life's purpose, for learning the lessons you were born with. By the way, you can't buy those either. You might regularly clip coupons from Safeway.com, but have you ever seen lessons listed there for a discount? You get what you pay for.

Appreciating the present may be a lesson in itself. There may be a better tomorrow, and there may not be, but what if you appreciated the here and now? Wouldn't that be something? Have fun for a change. It's out there to be had, in the present only, but it is up to you to take part in.

Be grateful for the totality of your life. Once you realize that *no one* is perfect, that's when you'll know you don't have to be, either. Life may be difficult and hard to accept. But lessons offer the most substantial possibility for change.

You do the same. Give yourself a break. Having it all is a notion devised by others, the media, and the agenda that goes along with it. You've achieved everything once you give credit to the lessons you learn; that's job number one.

Learning from others comes in handy here. Who do you learn from most? Friends? Family? Strangers? Those who are from your inner circle or out? At the same time I learned to welcome imperfection from Donny Osmond, another interview popped up. I was having an issue with the craft of writing, and suddenly, country singer Clint Black appeared on the TV talking about writing lyrics. He admitted that he makes regular use of a thesaurus when doing so. Thanks, Clint. If he can do it, so can everyone else. Again, I felt that I needed to be perfect until I realized I could be fallacious. Yes, that's a real word.

Mistakes are the antidote to perfectionism, so welcome them. Accept them; they happen to everyone. You learn from them. Maybe there's a lesson attached. Maybe not. Consider the

following examples:
1. You took the 10 heading west to Santa Monica at 5:00 PM on a weekday and imagined you'd zip right through. Once you became stuck in bumper-to-bumper traffic, you realized that it was just wishful thinking and not your instinct that told you to get on. While sitting and sitting, you were given a choice to either freak out or be patient and endure. You look around at others who are stuck because there's nothing else to do. You see their patience. They knew what they were getting into; you expected otherwise. Mistake. Common sense told you that you'd be stuck. If you'd have asked your instinct, you'd have proof that it prevails over wishful thinking every time. Nothing uncommon about it.
2. You've had friction with your neighbor for several months now about the loud music they play at all hours. You've tolerated it all along. Somehow, they've skirted the law by turning it down at 10:00 PM on the dot. No violation. It still bothers you; you become anxious and fearful every time you must "confront" them. When you do, it spurs them on, and they begin to act more and more irrationally towards you and the issue at hand. At around the same time, you find that your dog has become quite ill, and it dies unexpectedly. Did the neighbors poison it? No evidence to support that. Your instinct knows. You figure that karma will take care of everything. Nothing's changed. You want things to be mellow. Lesson: speak up, stand your ground. Don't expect karma to take care of what you're here to master. Don't take the law into your own hands, but stand up for what's right. Not doing so would be a mistake. Call out what's wrong, and don't settle for what you don't deserve.

3. For the last two years, you've questioned a particular friendship. Your gut tells you that it's a connection that's no longer equal. Jealousy may be at play. And your only reason for remaining in that friendship is because it's lasted nearly three decades. Loyalty. In those three decades, you've grown and changed into someone else. Your friend may have as well, but when you communicate with this old friend, you revert. You've gone back to giving, supporting, and accommodating when you know you shouldn't. You ignore your feelings and want to be perfect by being there for them, just as you always have. You don't call this friend, and how odd it seems. Every time this friend calls you, it's at the exact time you're in the bathtub, unable to take it. Then, another time, he calls you when you're on a nature walk. Are you going to interrupt your sacred alone time to take the call or not? You give thought to the dynamics of the friendship. You always ask, "How are you?" and you hear all about their life. You hear nothing supportive in return. Lesson: take loyalty and emotion out of the equation. You deserve nothing less than 50/50. There's a give and take to life. Always be open to receiving; you deserve it.

Looking In

Did you know that finding enjoyment by yourself is on the rise? In 2021, Google trend data showed that "Solo travel" has risen in popularity by 761.15 percent. The most common motivation for traveling solo is the wish to see the world without waiting on others.[12]

If you're not already doing so, create and cherish alone time. It works wonders. If you don't like being alone, don't fret.

You never are. Other folks are great for sharing lessons and giving and receiving them. It's a joint venture, but when it comes to learning *your* lessons, no one is ever going to be able to do that for you. You're on your own. And that's a good thing.

The benefits of alone time are endless, but the most obvious is seeing an unobstructed path filled with clear visions of you, what's on your mind, and how to solve all that's ailing you. When you're alone, giving yourself alone time, you're building your inner strength. You're reminded that you were put here to learn. When someone else's point of view is habitually around you, you see your own life through a filter. It's always clouded and camouflaged, like trying to have a good day when you're always hungover. Yikes! You never get past the fog.

Be brave and see through what you don't want to see (at this moment). For most, courage comes and goes, but when tackling the biggest lessons, you're more than ready for them when you move into your, and only your, perspective. Being away from others and their energy, for however long that may be, will fill your tank. It's a healthy balance, and when yours is full, you're ready to interact with others again. Still, leave their lessons to them. If they ask for your opinion, you can give it as long as you've already met your own needs.

Participate in social media only if you're doing it for the right reasons. Use it in moderation. Andrew Weinreich, who many consider the father of social networking, launched Six Degrees in 1997 to help people connect with others they haven't yet met.[13] That's awesome. For those who are able, I applaud the healthy way you've found to participate. I've already mentioned to you that it was unhealthy for me to be in the past, be reminded of it, and re-connect with friends where one of us has changed and done our work and the other has not. This was only one aspect of social media that was unhealthy for me.

If you're at all a giver or a pleaser, watch out! Social media can be a trap that's hard to escape. You've got to be very secure in who you are and what you're all about. Do you feel that when you like, comment, and share, you deserve the same back? Don't blame others for not reciprocating. Instead, monitor your amount of giving. You are responsible for 100 percent of your actions. If you're the least bit vulnerable in your identity, who you are, and what you're all about—if you post on social media to impress, boast, compete, seek validation, or attempt to make the past the present—then you should re-think your approach. All you're looking for in the real world is never going to come from an (electronic) social presence or any virtual reality.

Also, freeing yourself from social media usage liberates you and the time you have available for yourself. Have you ever temporarily deactivated your Facebook, LinkedIn, and/or Instagram accounts? Even a brief hiatus will allow you to focus on your own goals more exclusively. No, when you're a giver, this is not at all selfish. If you've got a secure sense of self, go for it! But remember, there's a great, big, real existence out there. Enjoy it now before it all becomes artificial.

A reprieve from social media also frees you up to meet new and different friends. Sometimes, as if by accident. In the real world—out on a walk, at the grocery store, the old-fashioned way. Do you think of yourself as old-fashioned? Try it. Initiate a conversation with a stranger somewhere, with no agenda attached, and see how mutually gratifying it can be. You'll be glad you did. Social media was supposedly created for *you*. If it no longer serves your purpose, create your own means to socialize. Out of nowhere, you're going to find that your need to be perfect will diminish greatly. You're going to veer back to the more authentic and truer you.

Suppress Predictability and *Get Unstuck*!

Nothing breaks you away from perfectionism more than thinking and acting outside the box. Whether made of cardboard or wood, get out right now! And do something differently! Do you think that you've now got it down to a perfect way of doing things? Then, you're too comfortable. You're not open to new and different, and you're pushing yourself further away from the new and different lessons headed your way. You haven't learned the old because you're stuck. Not in the present but in the past.

Starting now, how about doing just one thing differently? One. Maybe for less than a minute. It doesn't matter. Here are some quick and actionable examples:

1. Cook a meal you've never cooked before. For *yourself*. Not attached to an agenda.
2. Take a different route to the grocery store.
3. If you part your hair on the left, try the right for a change.
4. If you're compulsive about answering texts immediately, wait until it's most convenient for *you* to reply.
5. If you normally walk ten thousand steps per day, be satisfied with 7,500 one day instead, and don't feel that you've short-changed yourself.

Did you think of one thing? One is all it takes to get the ball rolling. Take it from them: rolling balls have credibility; they're *never* stuck. It certainly doesn't have to be action, either. Rather than doing something differently, how about changing up the way you think about something or someone? Again, a simple one. This is gonna change things up as well. If you're into this and like the feel, maybe you'll mix and match: a different way of thinking combined with a different course of action.

Again, you're trying these prompts out. They're low-risk and simple. You're doing this for a reason: getting unstuck may

involve learning a lesson or leading to the introduction of one. Examples:
1. When you're home at night, after a long day, reflect on *one* quality you like about someone that you find challenging.
2. Plan (in your mind) what it would be like to adopt a pet.
3. Think of someone who's inspired you or helped you in the past, and now think of the ways in which you're going to thank the next person who comes along and helps you out.
4. See yourself waking up, knowing that you "have it all." Nothing more is needed.
5. Think of all you've given out in life. Now, do the math. Don't you deserve something in return? The time's come for you to receive back all you've given out.

Keep It Simple

Keeping things simple doesn't mean aiming low. It's great to have high standards, believe in yourself, work hard, and shoot for the stars. Your life's purpose (life's lessons) will remain the same whether you achieve your goals or not. But going back to basics takes such a load off in addition to decreasing stress and adding to contentedness. It's so simple and easy. Lessons become more evident because there's less clutter surrounding them. Because they become so obvious to you, there's less time needed to decipher them. You learn them when you're able. When you're a senior individual, clocks tick louder.

No matter your age, mix it up. Instead of perpetual planning and programming, every once in a while, elect to think on your feet. It's great exercise. Burns calories, too. Nothing adds excitement to a sedentary life more than thinking and acting on the spot, learning lessons on the fly. It's kind of like catching a Frisbee in your teeth.

If you've still got a box, move it to the basement. At some point, when you add spontaneity to your diet, that container will become obsolete. Your pattern of doing the same old, same old will become destroyed, and you'll never go back. Think of that box as a trash can that you cannot wait to kick to the curb. Your GPS has been aiming you in this direction for ages. Why not listen to it for a change? Place your perfection(ism) into the trash, and don't feel compelled to replace any of what you've thrown out. More than likely, you've already got enough on your plate. No need for seconds. Light, simple, less cholesterol, and lowered blood pressure. A winning combination prescribed by Dr. You. And make certain that the prescription can be read legibly when requesting a refill.

Get unstuck! Any way you can! You're going to clearly see those lessons that have been disguised all those years. They're to be dealt with and learned from. Ending sentences with prepositions ain't right, but now, well into the sixth chapter of this book, I've just gotta mix things up before my brain goes soft. A condition that Viagra nor Cialis can cure.

More retirees now volunteer as a way of mixing things up. Of the nearly 25 percent of senior volunteers surveyed by the Center for Social Development at Washington University in St. Louis, 79 percent stated that they felt better about themselves, 95 percent felt that volunteering had enhanced their lives, and 96 percent said they had taken part in meaningful activities.[14]

Clearing the clutter is an inside job. It doesn't necessarily have to do with any box moving. Thinking too much and ruminating nonstop is as cruel as corporal punishment. It's estimated that between two hundred and five hundred million people meditate around the world. Meditation of any kind works wonders, and for the most part, it can be practiced while you're not even aware of doing it. I've been "meditating" in the bathtub for decades now. I just never knew it was meditation. If you're not a bath person, focusing your mind on nature while out on a walk will soothe you immeasurably. Overthinking means you've got to do whatever you can to unburden yourself of all the mental hoarding you're doing. Keeping your physical world plain and simple should be easy pickins, a no-brainer compared to a mind that can't be taken out for a walk.

Go out, way beyond that box. Find whatever nature you can come up with. Convenient, unassuming, safe, and with as few distractions as possible. When you immerse yourself in nature, you're letting go, freeing up, because you have, in essence, surrendered to something far greater that's outside of you. Nature is natural. It's untouched by man. Like Lady Gaga, it was born this way. Only a few minutes to start, and your mind will appreciate the attention you're bringing to it. No more neglecting the mental. Then, 30 to 45 minutes of devotion to something/anything outside yourself. A momentary gift to yourself, your mind, that yields hours of benefit.

Again, decluttering your mind = coming closer to getting unstuck. It opens a freer agenda upstairs. Let's face it, you're retired now. You've earned that white space within that full page. Enjoy it, and don't feel compelled to fill it in just because nothing's there. Your lessons are always with you, and they provide excellent company if you let them. Kind of like a best friend that happens to piss you off every other week. Grrrr.

The same goes for choosing friends. It's your choice. Drama queens are not royalty. They deserve no coronations and belong in only one palace: their own! They're great to learn from, but when you know they ain't never gonna abdicate, move yourself to another kingdom. Call Bekins or rent a U-Haul, relocate, and provide no forwarding address. If you've got friends or family who have not done their work but you have, good luck.

Or vice versa. Maybe they've learned their lessons, and you're not quite there. That's OK. Be grateful that there are friends in your life who know their lessons. Accept them and learn from them. See and appreciate the wisdom they've acquired. Be inspired by them and return the favor. Appreciate the education you've gained from them and see your own independent lessons for what they are.

Value what you learn from others and, most definitely, value what you've learned on your own. If you've chosen to integrate creativity or creative living, good for you. It's common knowledge that trauma survivors spend much of their early development (sometimes entire lifetimes) using only their left (survival) brains because they don't feel at liberty to make use of the other. Well, sometimes, it's a matter of mix and match. Living in reality is hard, whether you're still evolving or fully cooked. It's perfectly fine to write your own dictionary. One phrase I've always honored as a positive is "living in your own little world." What's wrong with that (within reason)? Whatever gets you from one day to the next warrants no comparison. Classic sitcoms got me through my childhood.

You're old enough to have watched *All in the Family*. Archie Bunker is a classic example of a living lesson (for us all). Simple, basic, and unpretentious, with a ton of lessons to learn. Not the most educated, but a *fantastic* teacher. Give thanks to Norman Lear. When you think of Archie and his unique sayings, try going all unsophisticated because he is. When you find yourself being too predictable, with too much on your mind, overthinking, and degenerating into perfectionist mode, go easy. Go wise because ~~you know~~ you've learned better. After Archie Bunker says, "Just don't do nothin' on the sperm of the moment," go spontaneous. When in doubt, laughing at Archie is like thanking him for showing us all the right way to do and think the opposite. We'd never be able to learn from Archie without accepting the humor he offers.

Earlier, we reviewed five ways to get unstuck involving action and thinking. Archie brings up another means: reaction. Here are five examples of getting unstuck by *re*acting in a new and different way. Again, they're simple, easy, and doable:

1. When someone at Home Depot helps deliver the potting soil to the trunk of your car, but some of the dirt spills out the tear in the plastic and onto the interior carpet, why not say, "Thanks. It's OK, no problem." It's carpet inside your trunk. (Who cares!?) Someone was helping you. Rather than criticize, accept and be thankful. No one's perfect.

2. You're headed to an Airbnb in the mountains, the perfect getaway. You arrive and find that there is no bathtub stopper, showers only. Taking a nice and relaxing bath is part of the plan. Instead of fretting, you shower instead, take up a fraction of indoor time, and hit the outdoors and experience one of the best days of your life. No luxurious, meditative bath, so what? You spent your time better than expected.

3. Your gut tells you that you just had the best audition of your life. Hiring that dialect coach really paid off. You compare yourself to the other actors who were at the casting, and your ego suggests that they couldn't have come close to what you accomplished there. You wait by the phone. It never rings. Time passes. You assume you did not get the role. You can't imagine who did. Your self-esteem begins to nosedive. You call your agent and ask, "Did they cast it?" Your agent says, "Oh, I guess I forgot to let you know. That project's off. Gotta go." This time, you realize that acting auditions, like life, is a numbers

game. Only fools take it personally. Attach yourself to nothing.
4. You travel crosstown for some vegan dim sum only to find that there is none. This was your mission, your objective, to order this specific item. Is there anything else on the menu that's vegan? Of course there is. Order from Column B instead. There are always options, sometimes much better ones. Substitute your first option with a surprise second, third, or fourth. And don't forget the fortune cookie that comes with it. Maybe it's vegan as well.
5. In a hurry, stuck in traffic on a two-lane highway, your blood begins to boil because you're going to be late for the start of the NBA Playoffs. You hear that an accident has occurred about a quarter mile ahead of you. When it begins to clear, other cars proceed ahead except for the car directly in front of you. You honk and can't understand why they aren't moving. There's no reaction from the driver, who has just had a heart attack. Instead of fixating on your agenda, you're thrust into someone else's. You learn patience and compassion firsthand, maybe for the first time. Big lesson.

Embrace the change. A host of scenarios have been presented to you. Did some resonate? Do any of the solutions appeal to you? Did you happen to notice how doing one thing differently equals the opportunity to grow, to learn a lesson, and doing what's been done before does not? This should come as no surprise to you at this point.

It could be fun to put into practice, don't you think? I think fools are onto something. They rush in, don't seem to be afraid of change or the unknown, and are rewarded with something new every time. Now, it's your turn. As a retiree, you've got wisdom on your side. So that means that you can play the fool without being foolish. Hard to predict if Mr. T will pity you or not, but that's *his* problem. Maybe he's jealous. No matter how many gold chains you happen to have hanging around your neck right now, go!

TAKE ACTION

- *Whether you feel you need to get unstuck or not, are you willing to do something different or differently every day?*
- *Even if it's the smallest of chores, ways of thinking, acting, or reacting, are you willing to commit to this change?*
- *Name a few of these modifications you're willing to make. List them and take action accordingly. You may learn something (new).*
- *If you chose to do something different, how did you feel? Before it? After it? Were you excited? Scared? Both?*

7

ACCEPTANCE

If you're not already doing so, this is where you'll learn to value suffering—your own and possibly that of others. Inspire them as they have inspired you. Accepting the way your life turned out takes a load off. It destroys the illusion of that perfect self you generated long ago. Mid-chapter, you'll study examples of outcomes that turned out better because of accepting mistakes as superior, surprise solutions.

You'll see virtue in accepting your purpose vs. disowning it. You'll be shown how accepting unjust circumstances and situations leads to peaceful resolution. Justice serves all inevitably; do all you can do, accept what you can't control, and move on. You'll be asked to accept yourself as you are, never settle for what you don't deserve, and always be open to better. Be grateful for everything in your life that's "as is."

The end of this chapter asks you to go beyond yourself to entertain the notion that there's something greater "out there." Begin in nature. Experience it. Enjoy it. Appreciate it. Think about a question you'd like answered as you partake or think of nothing at all. Let your mind go. Empty it. Then, move on to meditation if you're so inclined. It's as simple as walking in nature.

Change is inevitable. We grow, learn lessons, and do our best to fulfill our life's purpose, yet I now believe that we go out the same way we come in. We may be wiser when we leave, but the integrity of our souls remains unchanged. I'm grateful for this. When I look in the mirror, I fully take in what I see: a good person. Someone complex, but there's no doubt about it, a fundamentally good person throughout who's not perfect and at this stage is grateful for all the flaws as well.

Change is challenging. Do you welcome change? Or do you steer clear of it? A recent study by the Change Perception Index showed that one out of three people would avoid change if they could. Nearly two-thirds say that uncertainty about the future concerns them, but almost77 percent of people said they could be fearless in a particular situation if they needed to be.[15] How do you feel now that you're retired? Did you dread this day? Or are you open to new ways of living your life? New ways of feeling fulfilled?

If suffering is part of your transition, accept and appreciate it.

Value-Added Suffering

At the time of this writing, Spanish tennis player Rafa Nadal, at age 37, has hinted that this year, 2024, may be his last. He's about to retire and is planning a farewell tour. Nadal is one of the most tenacious, talented, and competitive athletes ever to engage in sport. Like myself, many have learned from him. A superstar athlete but an even better person. So many great qualities, yet there's one that stands out most: the value he places on pain and suffering. I've followed Rafa's career for many years, but it's not until recently I learned more about the "Spanish way" of viewing sports and competition. Those Spanish participants believe that suffering is necessary; it adds valor and is part of the process during a point, game, and match, during practice, and maybe even during the press conference that follows. Suffering is vital to the soul of the athlete and the sport involved. It validates the victory as well as the loss. The win is worth more when the player ~~feels~~ values their own anguish. A win is worthless if the player experiences no suffering en route to victory.

Yes, suffering is of tremendous value. What an interesting concept. More than "the pain is worth the gain," it's equal to it. What if we unconditionally accept suffering as part of the game? Our game? The game of life? Wouldn't that be something?

You have suffered. You may be suffering now. And, more than likely, you will suffer in the future. Do you see this as a positive? Or a negative? Does suffering add to your victories? Makes them more worthwhile? You're wise now and have learned moderation (perhaps a lesson of yours). As a retiree, keep up the balancing act. When life's too challenging, integrate something easy into your daily grind. Grind easier. When you do, you'll greet change with a grin vs. a grimace.

Join the crowd and be a happy retiree. In an article published by *New Retirement*, 76 percent of people aged 65-74 often feel happy. Compare that to only 51 percent of 25–34-year-olds. Just 47 percent of younger people say that they often feel content and happy, while 71 percent of those retired individuals report contentment.[16]

When I look way back now to the aftermath of my life-changing event in 1992, I was grinning because I was about to greet my writing idol, Alice Walker, the author of *The Color Purple* and so many other books, at a bookstore in Menlo Park, California. There, she appeared calm and quiet. She was marketing her new novel at the time, *Possessing the Secret of Joy*. I purchased it and listened to Ms. Walker speak from the podium, but it seemed that being in front of an audience was uncomfortable for her. After her talk, I stood in line and couldn't wait for her to sign my copy. The people before me offered chitchat stuff, and she said little in reply. "You inspired me to write," I told Ms. Walker. She looked up at me and offered me the biggest smile I had ever seen. I meant what I said, and I will remember that smile forever.

Alice Walker writes about suffering and the acceptance of it. That she is a spiritual person is quite evident in her books. Ms. Walker knows suffering, and the stories she writes have inspired and helped many to heal.

When I saw *The Color Purple* in the movie theatre in the mid-80s, my mind was too preoccupied to appreciate it. When I saw it during and after my life-changing moment, it led me to inevitably realize that everyone suffers. Suffering is an integral part of life. We choose to learn from it, or we don't. Every one of us has this powerful option. We can choose to learn the lessons that are given to us, or we can dismiss them and take them for granted. Think of that lotus flower in the mud. It may not have access to Botox, collagen injections, and personal trainers, yet it ends up coming out looking radiant and beautiful. No longer muck-encrusted, no evidence of mud at all. It's gorgeous on the outside and wise beyond measure within its core.

Although all lessons come custom-delivered, acceptance is ordered off the menu, especially in today's world. There are lots of opportunities to accept others and what they're all about. Remember my story having to do with learning about civil rights from the car radio? Well, I'd grown a bit older in the 70s and thought I'd become wiser. I recall my first time watching *The Jeffersons*, reflecting on Tom and Helen Willis. All that fuss about mixed marriages. Then, I thought to myself, someday, this won't be an issue at all because, at some point in history, we're all going to be fully mixed. Yale professor Stephen Stearns' research shows that globalization, cultural diffusion, immigration, and the ease of modern-day travel will steadily homogenize the population of humans, averaging out progressively more of people's traits.[17] Don't know exactly when "fully" is going to happen, in which century, but someday. Until that time, it is best to accept.

Just like characters in a sitcom, everyone's got a story. A backstory, maybe even a front and middle one, too. Some stories are well-hidden, and although others may appear out in the open, *never* assume. When a person offers you their story, listen. You'll more than likely learn from it, have a better understanding of that person, accept them for who they are, and hopefully feel compassion for them. Accept that some folks can't even own their stories; they're too painful and shame-filled. As you know, I perpetually ask "Why?" questions. If you're comfortable enough, ask someone you know why something happened or why they reacted in a certain way. You being all ears is their medicine. This doesn't mean you can play Dr. Phil because they're not asking your advice. Just listen and accept. If you've been critical of them and their actions, maybe their story will explain what really made them the way they are.

If you're brave enough to tell your story, don't expect others to comprehend. That's OK. What's unacceptable is their rejection of your truth. Friends from the past will see you the way they want to see you, no matter what, until they are open and accept, or they don't. You know my story. Some of you may wonder, "How do you know this really happened (since your parents never offered a full confession)?" This is OK as well. You only know my name as the person who's written all these words. The story sounds like science fiction to me as well, had I not lived through it. But, when you tell your story, your truth, and someone who's been a trusted friend asks, "So, you've got proof now? You're sure of this?" stop right there. These friends from the past are always going to see you through their vintage lens, see the you that you used to be (before your life-changer). And no amount of Windex is going to make it clear to them. If you eat, live, and breathe the truth and someone else doubts you and what you have to tell them, you deserve to have new friends.

Just like the mother yells out in *The Joy Luck Club*, "Know your worth!" Amen to that. If someone else, anyone else, questions you, doubts you, or doesn't believe you, this is *un*acceptable. They're reflecting their bias, not yours. Perhaps they live by different values than you do. Perhaps, for them, fibbing is the norm, and sincerity isn't valued. As mentioned previously, perhaps they have not done their work and view their own stories as fiction. That's OK (for them). Doing some friend-weeding could be a lesson of your own. Once you realize your worth, you accept nothing of inferior value in return. Leave cut-rate bargains to Costco.

You'll Never Walk Alone

Where were you when…? What do you do to feel comforted? Who or *what* makes you feel that you're never alone? Which place do you go to feel secure?

My default recommendation: back to nature. Yes, I'm going there (again). My go-to place 'til I die. I hope you see nature the same way. If you don't already, be open and…picture it. No, not Sicily, 1922, because I'm not Sophia Petrillo (although many have said we resemble each other). I've already told you about the comfort I felt accepting 9/11 in my little, removed life and what that was all about on my walk on the East Shore of Lake Tahoe the day that happened. Looking back, I knew I wasn't alone on that trail, though.

Every step I took, listening to the pebbles crunching under my feet, brought me closer to patience and acceptance—both at the same time. Patience, in general, grounds you. Patience in nature does more than that.

Nature's so much bigger than ourselves, our lives out there, out anywhere.

There are so many unique and different experiences available to us when we venture outdoors. All healing, all needed. Being in nature is an experience millions take part in daily that provides not only pleasure but also harvests medicine for the soul.

Whether you prefer walking through the forest or through the streets of midtown Manhattan, keep your eyes open. You'll be surprised by what they see. Although the movie *Midnight Cowboy* was rated *X* when it was first released, it seems like kid stuff now. Did you get a sneak peek when you were younger? Or did you have to wait until you were mature enough? Either way, you're sure to remember the famous line, "I'm walkin' here," uttered by one of the two main characters, Ratso Rizzo.

On movie sets, crews often have everything controlled to the last detail, mainly because delays cost production companies tons of money. No one wants that. Traffic control is one of them, but trying to control a crosswalk scene in midtown Manhattan? Get real. Cut (back) to that famous scene where Ratso (Dustin Hoffman) and Joe Buck (Jon Voight) cross a busy street. If you don't recall, do yourself a favor and Google or YouTube it. All in the scene goes as scripted until a not-so-patient taxicab driver chooses to plow through the pedestrians at a green light. Not only did Dustin Hoffman stay in character during this production flub, but so did Jon Voight, the extras, and everyone else on camera. Brilliant and unplanned. Spontaneous, improvised.

Accept all, control nothing. To think that we can control everything is laughable. Some may say that you can't control anything. Who knows? Where laughs are concerned, some of the biggest have come from improvisation. A writer scripts the story, but sometimes situations warrant a spontaneous reaction. Improv. If you haven't tried it, do. It'll get you through anything. And it oftentimes yields the best results. In your own life, keep the cameras rolling because you never know what's going to unfold before your eyes.

How many times have you improvised in life? Fun, ain't it? More than fun, it is a fantastic opportunity to share, participate, and make better. In business, life, and improvised comedy, "Yes, and" gives us a chance to take in an idea, circumstance, or information that's thrown our way and add to it. A creative edit to living in a practical world. You've got to agree on one thing: sometimes chance outcomes turn out far better than anything that could have been intended. Accept these surprises. They are gold. In the bigger picture, there's presumably a lesson or two involved. Planning out the same old, same old keeps us stuck. How can we learn lessons when we perpetually place ourselves within these self-imposed rigors of planning? It's nearly as bad as perfectionism. It's not at all distasteful to inspect your own behind every once in a while, to see if there may be a stick up there. Ouch! If so, remove it and keep walking.

Accept Your Purpose

Whether you want to or not, accept what you're meant to learn, even if the truth embarrasses you or sheds light on what your ego doesn't want to admit. Accept and deal with it. Sometimes, full acceptance of the truth can be a lesson in itself. If you're perfectly fine blaming your misfortunes on having been raised by a narcissist until you realize for certain that you are one yourself, accept responsibility.

Over time, the more you're able to accept (and appreciate) your past, the easier forgiveness becomes. As a matter of fact, it becomes so easy that you'll ultimately choose to do it for yourself as well. A win-win. Accept-accept.

Accept yourselves for who you are and why you're here. Admit it. Hey, as a mature citizen of the world, when you view your reflection in the looking glass, what could you possibly see that you haven't already seen before? No, not wrinkles. While you take it all in, don't examine your past in detail because you ain't there anymore. View it abstractly. The current *you* came from somewhere, and you must have learned something to get from A to B to C or D or whatever letter you're up to by now. Live in the S or T of life; the rest of the alphabet will come to you when you're ready. Study that face and accept all that's behind it. Don't forget, you're the one who designed your book cover. No one else did. Make sure others can read the real story.

Karma's a spiritual thing, right? Well, I'm all for it. God/The Universe/Your Higher Power will right wrongs via karmic justice. But as we get older, we're reminded more and more that we're here as spiritual beings living as humans on *Earth*. *Human* beings. We have to do *our* part *here*. How do you see us? In my eyes, no matter which country you live in, the justice system is here for a reason. Seeking justice is doing *our* part. Human beings doing what's humanly possible. What happens beyond that may be out of our control, but we may have a hand in lighting a fire under karma's ass.

Looking back a few years to the People v. O.J. Simpson trial, many suffered and continue to do so because of the slayings of Nicole Brown Simpson and Ron Goldman. Everyone watched the trial and reacted to the verdict. After its conclusion, daytime programming went back to soap operas, talk shows, and game shows. Back to normal, except for the families of those victims. Oh, the pain they felt then and continue to feel. Then, a bit of time passed. Both families were still in the news, always being interviewed. There was even one very public, prominent talk show host who'd asked Fred Goldman (Ron Goldman's father) as diplomatically as possible, "Wouldn't it benefit you most to…move on?" IMO, that wise person asking the question didn't get it right. Perhaps she didn't know that the actualization of justice may have been a lesson for Mr. Goldman and the Goldman family. Justice for victims was and is wildly important. Seeking it, attaining it, may have been a vital ingredient for karma to commence.

    As you might know, the Goldman family did not let it go. They proceeded with civil litigation against O.J. Simpson and won. It's referred to as a judgment, a monetary victory, but *way* more important, it's called justice. Justice for the victim(s). This is what it's all about. If I had a child that was murdered, I would do whatever it took to make sure justice happened for my child. Through the legal system, of course. Never self-police.

    A few years passed, and as we all know, O.J. was arrested in Las Vegas for robbery, found guilty of twelve charges, and was incarcerated for several years. The Goldmans were not involved in this criminal trial, but I wonder if they view it as karma, something that happens independently of what we humans do, though we do play a part in its emergence. The Goldmans sought justice for their son, and they got it. I'd do the same.

    I'm a justice junkie and watch *DATELINE* religiously, almost every day. I empathize with those families that have lost loved ones and continue to suffer. Some are so determined to keep pushing for justice, pushing that lead detective to do more before all turns cold. Good for them! In these episodes, as the challenging hunt for evidence is driven to proceed, lucky breaks happen seemingly out of nowhere. Hold it a second! Nowhere? Are you kidding me?! They happen because those families are pushing so tirelessly, or the detectives are doing a bit extra while seeking justice.

Anyone would feel for those families. Sometimes, the verdicts go the way they want, and sometimes they don't. Even with guilty verdicts, the victim's families often say the same thing, "I was still left empty, not as good as I thought I'd feel. It doesn't bring _____ back." I can understand and empathize, but if only they could see these trials through the victim's point of view, even for a fleeting moment. Difficult, I'm sure. Trials exist because of injustice(s), and innocents become victims as a result of this injustice. A guilty verdict means victory and justice for the victims who are no longer around to defend themselves. It's all about *them*, their redemption. *Their* lives mattered. These justified guilty verdicts validated *them* and their lives (and deaths). Justice for the victim usually elicits karma all over the place. I don't know how, why, when, or where, but look for it because it's out there somewhere.

When I used to write middle-grade novels, my challenged young protagonist would always say, "If you take the first step, God will take the second." Maybe childlike Miguelito wanted to cut corners and just expect, but his wise Aunt Shirley told him that God doesn't work that way. What you expect you will not have. Bingo. We've all learned this by now, haven't we?

I'm all for living a spiritual life, but once more, we're here on Earth, not in Heaven (yet). It's time to get real and do our part. I recall that advice Aunt Shirley had given to Miguelito when I used to chat with a co-worker, Marcus. He was so wise, graduated from a theological seminary, and earned his Ph.D. His department happened to have an opening for an upgraded position coming up soon. Marcus would tell me how much he wanted it. In the beginning, I'd say to him, "That's great. What are you doing to get it?"

"I pray every day," Marcus responded.

"Oh, awesome. What else? Schmooze?"

"I'd been thinking about submitting my resume and application. I pray…all the time."

I didn't have much to say after that. Was Marcus doing all he could? Or was he expecting? I admired Marcus, and I respected his prayers. They meant so much to him. End of discussion.

Everyone's got different philosophies, and that's the way it's always going to be. For me, it's always going to be: We're here to learn lessons. We're here to make things happen for ourselves, to know our worth, and live our power. If we get an assist, it is icing on the cake. Just ask Betty Crocker.

Accept All

Accept responsibility for your life—all you want to learn, enact, do, and change. Don't expect; instead, accept. You can certainly control your desires and effort, but you can't control outcomes. And you know why that is. It's because you cannot alter the lessons that are given to you. They're provided to you for a precise reason. Accept them as they are, and you'll be better able to sleep at night and go on to live a fulfilling life. You're living your purpose when you accept all that's been given to you.

Accept that you're a retiree. It's an honorable term. It means that you've done something. You've worked at something, and now you're changing positions. You're transitioning. Don't be in denial about the term retirement. Just as a job was not your identity, neither is retirement. Neither are you. Retirement's just a word.

Not until my 60s did I begin to accept *all*. Others may call this surrendering to God. I'll buy that. This was the magic decade when I shifted my entire outlook and eliminated expectations once and for all. Plain and simple, I accepted everything about me, my life, and the way everything has panned out. I found out that it's not a matter of accepting that certain long-held goals are never going to be achieved; it's more a matter of accepting that—over time—they have been replaced by something much greater. Accepting some greater plan changed my life forever.

Do you believe there's a greater plan? Something you could have never devised yourself? Do you accept it? Or do you abide by yours alone?

Now, at 66, instead of thinking that so many things have passed me by, I realize that I haven't missed a thing. I'm far richer than I ever would have imagined. I've accepted all.

I've also accepted that I may never be fully understood by anyone. It's a narcissistic trait to think this way, by the way. It doesn't deter me from accepting others as is, no matter if I understand them or not. Judging others took up so much space inside my head. It's something I continue to work on, but I acknowledged and accepted that this was one of my main lessons from long ago. As a result of judging others less, I am less critical of myself. I don't necessarily feel love, but I'm grateful to feel anything at all—compassion, understanding, sincere awareness of backstory, fondness, and affection. It's wrong to even consider these feelings as substitutes. They are what they are. I am what I am. You are what you are. Accept everything.

When you're a senior, you haven't missed a thing. We all remember Maxwell Smart from *Get Smart* and how he perpetually "missed it by that much," but when looking back, we knew him when he must have been about 40 or so. Yes, I'm talking about a fictional character who talked into a shoe. Forty-year-olds don't know as much as us. When you're in your forties, you may feel as if you've missed opportunities or missed "having it all" by "this much." Now, who the hell wants it all? That concept is as fictitious as Agent 86. Plus, Don Adams was always much more credible as Tennessee Tuxedo. Right?

Don't compare yourself to anyone ever. Erase societal standards and live by your own instead. The same goes for your internal resume. When you read yours, see unequivocal success. Seeing the lessons you've chosen to tackle, from start to ~~finish~~ now, I'd hire you in a second. Be your own master, if you will. It's all in how you see yourself and what you're all about. Change your perspective, and it will change how you see yourself. Focus on all you've learned, the wisdom you've acquired, and you'll recognize that you're an overachiever in what some may call the *non*physical world. A place you'll *never* find on MapQuest.

Are you more into accepting yourself as is? There's a lot there, let me tell you. Sixty-six don't come easy. And never consider any of what you've brought along with you as baggage; carry-ons sound so much nicer. Like I'd said, for so much of my life, I thought "lessons" were synonymous with "duties, obligations, commitments made that yield no rewards." Wrong. Once you recognize that lessons = life's purpose, the magnitude of the word becomes evident. They are *the* reason you're here—to learn something specific. Do you want to take on the job and do whatever it takes to succeed undeniably? Or just half-ass it?

Changing your point of view changes everything! Do you feel as if you've missed out on anything? A long-held desire of yours that turned out to be a "What was I thinking?" Letting go of outdated, obsolete desires = maturity and growth, and usually involves having learned a lesson or two while en route to your increased level of wisdom. Hey, if you've got one, take a look at a to-do list you made when you were in your 20s or 30s. All that's left undone was perhaps left that way for a reason. It was replaced by a lesson. Let's take a look at some examples.

To Do: (Age: 20s/30s)	Lesson: (Mature adulthood)
• Go out with Joe HotBody. He's a player, but, *damn, he's fine!*	• You've learned your worth. Let Joe play; you can play with yourself.
• Live in the suburbs, have 2.5 children, and make sure they get into USC or Stanford.	• Happiness only comes from within. Doesn't matter where you live. Cherish numbers one, two, and three (or any fraction thereof) equally. Give them freedom.
• Start dating after losing twenty pounds.	• Healthy relationships exist only when you love yourself 20 pounds over, under, or as is. "As is" isn't "good enough," it's just right, Goldilocks.
• Find someone to write the "story of my life."	• You ended up writing it yourself after you realized no one else could do the job justice.
• Giving to others is a Christian act.	• So is giving to oneself.

Before and after to-do lists = report cards for adults. Always an *A* for effort, never a need to forge your mom or dad's signature. Did you ever do that? Or were you proud to show off your grades? As a kid, I had little confidence because I didn't know any better. When you feel confident, you know you're living your life's purpose because there's some lesson attached. Knowing your power and living it may not be a lesson for everyone, but it certainly has been for me.

Life's lessons come about because we're born with them. But as kids, we're taught lessons by our teachers in school. In my childhood, I liked certain subjects more than others, but my favorites were foreign languages, for sure. Routinely, I got Cs, Bs, and Ds across the board in all subjects. Again, I didn't know any better, and I accepted my fate. I was meek, overweight, and afraid to open my mouth most of the time. Like life, I was going through the motions of being a student until…

One day, the classroom was silent. Everyone, including me, was focused on taking a test. Seated in the back row behind everyone else, I was doing my best to concentrate. Our teacher, Frau Volkmann, quietly walked through the room, monitoring us. She stopped at my desk. She stooped over and crouched down to my level. What had I done wrong? I wasn't cheating. What did she want?

In a whispered tone, Frau Volkmann began to speak, "Clinton, I've been talking to Ms. Robson (my social studies teacher), and we both believe you should be getting As."

I was speechless. What did this have to do with the German test I was taking? I said nothing in return.

"You're smart. You should be getting As."

Although I didn't know what to make of Frau Volkmann, I knew she was being for real. She looked like she cared about me. The only response I remember making was an affirmative nod. I never told anyone about that interaction, but I'll remember it forever. More than any foreign language, math, science, English, or P.E. class, that one-minute speech Frau Volkmann gave me during that German exam was the most important thing I ever learned in high school because I'm still learning it.

I had accepted living in the shadow of everyone else. I had accepted being quiet. Frau Volkmann made sure I knew that I mattered. After my interaction with her, getting *A*s became commonplace. I still had difficulty with math, but I applied myself anyway. Frau Volkmann changed my life. The next year, as a junior, I lost sixty-plus pounds and found that I enjoyed playing sports, especially tennis. All of this was new. Coming out of my shell seemed to happen naturally, and I accepted the me that had been waiting to emerge.

I love people, but part of me will always need my shell. A few years ago, I Googled Frau Volkmann so I could offer an extremely overdue "thank you." I shouldn't have been surprised to find on the Internet that other former students had done the same. Now, my turn. I composed my note of gratitude and sent it off via Facebook Messenger but didn't receive a reply for several months. Apparently, her infrequent logins on social media mirrored mine. Frau Volkmann told me what she's up to now, where she is, and a little about that time of her life. She mentioned that she remembered me. When I read that, I felt validation all over again. Everyone who's made such a dramatic impact on your life deserves recognition. Although I accepted my life as is, I accepted it because I didn't know any different. Frau Volkmann (and Ms. Robson) didn't accept me as is because they had seen me as much better.

How about you? Who's your Frau Volkmann? Is there someone who was or is in your life that made you see yourself differently? If there's any doubt in your mind that you may have taken them for granted, then...

Take action. It's easy to do. It's easy to assume they know

they did good, but show it! This doesn't mean you're out to add a new social media connection. Do more than that. Something meaningful. Summon your gratitude, and don't be afraid to express all of it. Find that person and let them know their actions and their concern for you was and is appreciated. Do this via any means you choose (writing, phone, or in person). Make it known that they mattered to you, and still do. Good job! *A+!*

Acceptance-to-Gratitude

Maybe they're related, maybe not. Acceptance and gratitude are their own entities, but when combined, look out! Get ready to go to the next level. Accepting others, yourself, conditions, and circumstances and being at ease with all is great. Accepting what you'd previously perceived as adversity, poor luck, or ill timing as being equally as great is fantastic. But it becomes wisdom when you not only accept but feel gratitude for it all, for everything. This is when you know for sure that your Plan A, Plan B, and Plan C mean nothing compared to the plan(s) you were born with. Yours are noble and serve a purpose but presumably involve doing, achieving, and accomplishing, not learning. When you accept the plan you were born with as the ultimate plan for you, you're living your purpose. Turning that acceptance into gratitude makes you a master. If you're not there yet, prep for it.

TAKE ACTION: Part 1
Now, it's your turn. Walk in nature, preferably alone (only when in a safe environment). It's a great place to reflect on repeat "coincidences" OR to seek solutions.
- *Is there a particular question you'd like answered about*

your life that's pertinent to your own lessons?
- *Does that question happen to relate to your own individual purpose within your life? How so?*
- *As you take your first steps, formulate a question you'd like answered, then ask it quietly.*

After about thirty minutes, your remedy will be inside your head simply because you'd inquired in solitude (with no distractions, clutter, or uninvited agendas).
- *At the end of your walk, realize that you just had a superb experience in nature – Appreciate it!*

TAKE ACTION: Part 2
- *Meditate by yourself or with others so your mind and body will be still and calm.*
- *In your imagination, try revisiting your favorite spot in nature, perhaps where you'd previously been on a walk or hike.*
- *This is a second opportunity to grasp the answers that were originally provided during your walk. Absorb them thoroughly, then put the solutions into practice.*

8

GRATITUDE

This chapter begins with the most obvious observation: the more you're grateful for, the more you realize you have. You're starting off your retirement knowing that you have everything you need and more to initiate the newest phase of your life. And the greatest earned asset to be grateful for, that only age can bring: wisdom. Wisdom = lessons learned. A possession you've netted by having worked hard. Here, you'll also learn to be grateful for the smallest of things and appreciate them the same as the greatest, wisdom.

Mid-chapter, you'll look back to lessons learned and be grateful for the challenging lessons in equal amount(s) to what you actually learned from them. You'll be encouraged to open up, trade anecdotes, and be grateful that you have the opportunity to inspire others via your share. It takes only one storyteller to get the ball rolling. There's no shame in being vulnerable.

Be grateful for your instinct because it's never wrong. When you learn in this chapter to be grateful for everything, you're opening yourself up to having it all. Be grateful for 100 percent of your past, present, and future. Grateful for who or what helped get you from A to B. At the end, you'll be asked to list all you're grateful for and all you may take for granted. You'll also be asked to evaluate your own instinct and mention the ways in which it helps you.

*I*n the "What Now?" growth scheme, gratitude = graduation. Once you're truly grateful for all, you're free from your past and fully present. Be grateful for what got you to where you are today. Say thanks every day for the totality of your life, the entire 100 percent of it. To become a senior individual means you've advanced several grades in the School of Life; you wouldn't be here today had you elected to drop out.

At this stage, it's only a disservice to look back. You've done this already countless times; you've worked through immaturity and learned your lessons. Little surprises you now because you've been there and done that. You now welcome the unknown because you see it as a new lesson to learn. What could be better?

To remain fully grateful, practice daily. The benefits of doing so are countless, but there are a quick six you can measure on two hands right now. According to Visiting Angels in Sarasota, Florida, a senior home care center, the six profits of practicing gratitude for seniors are:
1) Improves health
2) Strengthens relationships
3) Expands life's meaning
4) Improves memory
5) Increases spiritual connection, and
6) Builds self-esteem[18]

Any more you can think of? Which do you feel is most significant to you?

Take time out to think, pray, meditate, and make your

gratitude known, even for what you or others may think of as insignificant. The moment you regard anything you have been given as insignificant is the moment it will be taken away. Why should you be given more of anything if you are not grateful for what you have? Practice gratitude today! I mean it! If this isn't a ritual for you already, make it one. Nothing's too small, and *everything* has meaning.

Count Your Blessings (Literally)

For me, expressing gratitude mostly occurs in the middle of the night. And it happens quite naturally. Every night over the last few years, I have been fortunate enough to sleep in a bed with clean sheets, pillows, and blankets. In a safe bedroom. Sometimes with a TV in it. Sometimes, I cannot get over how lucky I am to have these things. Grateful, to be most precise. Thankful for these things because there was a time when I had none of them.

Do you have a room that provides safety and security? Are you grateful to be able to sleep in it regularly? Nighttime bears reflection; use that time wisely. You have countless hours to count your blessings.

In 2007, I lived in a homeless hotel at Polk and Broadway in San Francisco. I tried my best to get a job, make a living, and become financially independent from my mother cold turkey, but I didn't succeed. No clean bed, sheets, or blankets. It was not safe. My wallet was stolen. I had no money and fresh bedbug bites on both calves every night. Challenging then, grateful now. That time of my life taught me humility, and I am overflowing with gratitude for having all I felt I was lacking then. That time of my life taught me that we are all the same; none of us any better than the other. In that place, I wasn't afraid; I was doing my best to survive—just like everyone else. Compassion began entering my life then, but I had neglected someone in my practice: me.

While learning humility, I felt it prudent to help others. I recall one guy in that place asking if he could borrow $5 from me. I gave it to him on the condition that he pay it back; I had so little for myself. He never did, and it made me angry. I had put myself last, like I had done so many times before. I didn't learn it then, but it was a lesson in the making: compassion for myself. Years later, I learned not to give to anyone before giving to myself first. I'm grateful to have learned so many lessons that were born during that winter in San Francisco. And although dismal, my little room possessed a peekaboo view of the bay, the Golden Gate Bridge, and Alcatraz Island. Go figure. Not so shabby in the abstract, yet unworthy of a TripAdvisor review. Either way, I'm grateful for all I learned and the related lessons that followed.

Do you put yourself first, first? Sometimes? Always? Never?

The point of the story: When I wake in the middle of the night, I wake up in a clean, bug-free, safe, and peaceful place. To not be grateful for that every night would put me under that 100 percent. Get it? I'm still not good at math, but I'm grateful to be living at a time when my laptop is.

Now, how about you? Did I get you thinking about those little things that you often take for granted? Don't forget that nothing is exempt from gratitude. If you'd like more examples, here goes:

- Your socks don't have holes in them today.
- You remembered to take your vitamins.
- You no longer notice noises that used to bother you.
- There's still some tread left on your rear tires.
- After a horrendous fall, you notice that you *didn't* break a hip.
- Your young child comes home to you after school.

- No summer vacation this year, but you *can* camp out in your backyard.
- Sparky has no fleas.
- You chose not to retaliate when you easily could have.

There are millions, aren't there? Well, don't overdo it. Stagger your thanks. In the middle of the night, when you can't sleep, express what comes to mind first. And limit what comes next. If you go on and on and on, you'll never enjoy a good night's sleep, and nobody wants that. Instead, say thanks in your dreams. It still counts.

When it comes to giving thanks, size doesn't matter, and nothing's too obvious. Routinely, thanks are attributed to having good health, food on the table, clothes on your back, and money in the bank. Tried and true. All good. Even more meaningful when you've had none. The trick is to be just as grateful if you have or have not. If you don't have it when you think you should, do an inventory; you've got something else in its place. In 2007, when I had not, I had a lesson. A lesson that lives with me today. I'm never lacking anything because I have so much. Are you contemplating your haves? Do they equal or surpass your have-nots?

No matter your situation, there is much to be grateful for. Be grateful for what you *do* have because there's lots more to come. The minute you surround yourself with gratitude for all, you open yourself up for more. In essence, you've *made* this happen. You realize you've been living this life for a purpose, the most meaningful reason for your existence. One leads to the other. Gratitude is the penultimate realization. When you've got this, look out because surprises are in store. There's only one thing…

Never expect! You will absolutely never have what you expect or what you feel you deserve in a particular fashion. Blessings do come to you, but usually with a twist. A lesson may

or may not be involved with it upon delivery. Expectations lead to the opposite of gratitude: assumption, disbelief, unlikelihood. Do your very best to never have expectations. Instead:
- Learn your lessons.
- Do your work.
- Make things happen.
- Believe in yourself while doing so.
- Let it go.
- Be grateful for the opportunity.
- Be grateful you're still around.
- Be grateful if you get your desired outcome.
- Be grateful if you don't.

Every day, a little at a time, do your best to let go of any and all expectations (once and for all). The best reminder that comes to mind: Shania Twain. Remember her story? To this day, she's very much relevant, decades after her initial success. Again, I don't know her, nor am I familiar with her lessons (no one but Shania is). All I know is that she's been very open about expectations and reactions. Shania seems like a very hard worker; she's re-invented herself a time or two (which is awesome, by the way). Good for her. Change is good. New success has come to her via new generations of fans. I'd imagine, decades ago, she expected none of this. Believing in herself probably solidified her destiny and all the success she's achieved.

How different Shania's life might have been had she held on too tightly to her expectations. Just like all of us, Shania has seen some very challenging times (aka "lessons"). If I were to ever meet her, I'd be compelled to ask, "What did they teach you? What did you learn from them exactly?" In my imagination, I speculate her saying, "Expressing gratitude for all means being grateful for *every* lesson within my life, no matter how trying they may be, no matter how trying they have been. They bore my purpose." Well, maybe Shania wouldn't use the word "bore," but it sounds good to me. Not to put words into Shania's mouth, but her fantasy words are the exemplar of the point I'm trying to make. Others don't impress me much.

The lesson of acknowledging and expressing gratitude is universal. There cannot be one person alive who is immune to this lesson. Lessons are our life purpose, and they = growth, advancement, wisdom, and, yes, more truth. Truths we weren't aware of. Truths about ourselves, others, our changing desires, our needs, our situations, and our past. The way we look at things.

When we are grateful for all, we see our whole life story with 100 percent truth, the truth we know, because we are now open to it all. When reflecting on my own mom and dad, I see all of them. I find goodness and a host of admirable qualities. I recognize gratitude in their being my parents, and I feel gratitude in my being their son. In addition, I see two twenty-somethings. I see their joy and their pain. I feel compassion for what they must have gone through in their lives. I don't know their truths because I am not them, but I'm grateful for what I do know and for what I feel about them. I am so grateful to both my parents for being who they are and the lives they've chosen to live. Like all of us, me included, they made mistakes. Who doesn't? They were new to parenting and were maybe caught up in a moment. Again, I don't know. The details of it all don't matter now. None of them. I'm grateful for all.

Through my mother, I was raised to be kind, considerate, and show respect, just as she is, just as she does. I learned from her stellar example and wouldn't have it any other way. Decades have passed; I'll never know who may have been jealous of whom during that winter of 1991 because I no longer care. Those interrogations back then were eventually replaced with understanding and appreciation. My parents created in me a soul that's hungry for wisdom. Thanks, Mom (and Dad), for placing such a delicacy on my plate.

Because of my mother and father, I was introduced to a word I hadn't known before—compassion— and was given an entire lifetime to define it. They are good people. My mother and father gave me life, and equally important, they provided me with lessons. Lessons that have lasted sixty-plus years. Their lessons gave me the opportunity to be free. Lessons of overcoming dependency and insignificance I fought hard to learn. Like myself, always be open and ready for what's yet to be, but know it'll never arrive if you are not grateful for 100 percent of your past and present. You can't be grateful for your future because it hasn't happened yet. And never expect that you will be because expectations of any sort erase growth.

Triggers come up all the time; they're supposed to. They're part of the process, for sure. The lessons learned have so much to do with the new and different ways in which we react to triggers. Throughout all, keep your emotions in check. Leave all live wires to electricians. They deal with them for a living. Be grateful for triggers. I mostly associate them with what I'd called do-overs. They're grand opportunities to do better, to learn a lesson you may have let slip through your fingers.

What do you do when a trigger arrives? Hide under the covers? Or work through the lesson attached to it?

Go Deep(er)

There are times to live on the surface and times to do more than that. Consider that lotus flower. See them everywhere, even if they haven't sprouted yet. They're growing, changing, and ultimately blossoming. They're there for you to notice. What they're all about and where they came from. A natural occurrence.

Something to be admired and be grateful for.

Before late 1991, I used to be extremely sociable. Lighthearted, if you can imagine. Had *tons* of friends. My focus was on fun and doing my best to be funny. I was in my thirties, and maybe this is what you do at that age. Did you? At the end of that year, that all stopped, and I've never really gone back. At this point in my life, I somehow see fun as a luxury. It's not at all a focus of mine now, yet I do my best to integrate it into my life the best I can.

You're born to ~~please~~ do as you please. If your focus is on fun, great! If not, that's great too. One of my favorite words in Italian is "bilanciata," meaning balanced; a balanced load. A balanced life. According to the United Nations Population Division, Italy has the second largest share of people over 65, behind Japan as number one.[19] At a time, for the first time in history, most people (everywhere) are expected to live into their 60s and beyond. I can't speak for Italians as a whole because everyone is different, but I *am* qualified to mention what I noticed when I moved there in 2004. The Italians I saw placed extreme value on socializing. Other people, interaction. They all seemed to connect to each other so easily. For me personally, it was just what the doctor ordered at that time. Fun and light.

How balanced are you? Your life? Do you favor fun over "its opposite?" The most common antonym for fun is boredom. Let me tell you something: a deeper view of life and the life you're living is *not* boring! It's the total opposite. A mix of both is the winning formula, for sure. Maybe lessons can be learned from both. Maybe fun is the thing we embrace when we can't handle lessons 100 percent of the time. Maybe it's its antidote.

Bottom line: a healthy life is learning lessons part of the time and having fun for the rest of it. Another good word, "superficiale." A cognate, so no need to explain. The opposite of deep. On the surface. A horrid place to be, inauthentic. Not the truth. Not the true person. It's our purpose to look deeper when meeting people. They may not divulge their truth immediately or ever. Accept them for who they are and be grateful for your shared acquaintance. A joy to be had for the moment, but...

Superficial only goes so far and, in most cases, leaves you feeling *very* short-changed any time you encounter it. You've got a winning exchange if you come upon a "what you see is what you get" kind of person. Authentic, real, genuine, truthful. Superficial exchanges are also draining because so much time is wasted on both sides. "We're here for such a short time" is not just a cliché; it's reality. Most of the people we meet in life come to us in fleeting increments. Most never become lifelong friends, relationships that last and last. We should value these people as much as any others. Fleeting chance run-ins stem from the same origins as any other meeting(s); they are meant to be. When you meet a stranger, make the most of it.

Never be afraid of divulging TMI. Boundaries are great, but holding back is not. You are meeting these people for a reason. Maybe you can help them, maybe vice versa, and it's never by coincidence.

How often do you spill the beans? And make sure to listen carefully when others do—they're never spilled accidentally.

I've had a million of these interactions, and I never take any for granted. During the spring and summer, over 20 years ago, I used to regularly go to the Silver Terrace Cemeteries in the high desert of Virginia City, Nevada (just on the other side of the mountain from Lake Tahoe). There, I'd sit on a tucked-away bench and write (longhand) a book about being unafraid of dying, targeted for young readers. Every time I walked to and from that bench, I'd study those vintage Wild West headstones from the 1800s. Many, many children had died there during those years in

Virginia City, a city that rivaled San Francisco in its heyday. What was inscribed on those headstones was so profound, I thought. Poetic. Written in a way I'd never known before. I wanted to copy their words verbatim but didn't know if it was legally possible. I wanted to include them in my book as a tribute to those same children who had inspired me (via their gravesites). There's no way I was ever going to forget the names of these kids I'd only know by the presence of their headstones. I wanted to honor them.

I entered the full text of many headstones in my book, and then I began to worry about plagiarism. Were those words in the public domain? Or was I breaking the law? On my return from Virginia City—over the hill—one day, I headed back to my nearby home of Lake Tahoe to take a walk on a forested trail. Immediately after parking my car on the side of the highway, I was greeted by two tourists who'd asked me a touristy question. We chitchatted for less than a minute, then I asked the husband, "What do you do?"

"I'm a copyright attorney."

Are you freaking kidding me!?! A solid gold opportunity. I didn't want to intrude by asking a work-related question when he was off the clock. He graciously indulged me, though. He told me that the text on those headstones was too brief and too old to be an infringement violation of any type. Public domain. Free to reprint. Whew!

When I drove home, I couldn't believe my luck running into him. But, if you think about it, things like this happen all the time. I got an answer because I asked. Make sure you ask tons of questions. Be bold. If you're comfortable enough and you sense the other person is as well, ask why questions. Those are the best because they cultivate wisdom. When a tourist comes up to you and asks, "Where's the nearest toilet?" or "How do I get to _____?" go deep. There's more to the story. You're meeting for a reason that may or may not be arbitrary. Make it count, acknowledge their presence, and thank them for the conversation and for brightening your day.

Begin this new practice of yours today.

The Biggest Intangible

People, places, and things. Most typical tangibles are perceptible by touch. Early on, you re-defined "life's purpose." When thinking about assets, accomplishments, and achievements (the old definition of "life's purpose"), why not be grateful for them, as well? For me, it goes without saying that—most days and most nights—I see "lessons learned" as tangible. They are so ever-present in my mind that it's next to impossible for me to think otherwise. It's never gonna happen. You don't need to think of them as one way or the other. I just want to make you aware that there's a ton out there to be grateful for that's not provable, palpable, or evidentiary.

It doesn't matter (for the moment) whether you see lessons learned, to learn, or to be learned as something provable. You know why? There's something even greater out there to be grateful for. An assist, company, helper, companion, ~~party planner~~, and more. Something we were all born with, no exception. I know you're expecting me to work in the l-word (lessons) here because it sure sounds like I'm about to, but seriously, there's another word that fits the bill in the same way. Something I never dismiss or take for granted and always appreciate. Ready for it?

Instinct. If ever there was a gift we should never re-gift, it's this one. To many, it's the most powerful asset we have hanging from our toolbelt. Trust me. It's never wrong, and it's wildly underutilized. Sometimes, it needs sharpening, especially when it's been neglected for too long. Like a muscle, the more you work it, the stronger it becomes. A shame its existence cannot be proven. But, damn, there sure are a lot of synonyms created for something that (some believe) may or may not exist: intuition, gut feeling, sixth sense. And, no, I'm not talking about *Basic Instinct*; I'm talking about something entirely different. That movie did, however, teach me to always wear underwear whenever I happen to cross my legs.

Because instinct is something that cannot be proven, there are so many interpretations of what it is exactly. What about you and yours? Are you one who gives credence to instinct? Or do you dismiss it? In Britain, two thousand adults were surveyed, and about seventy percent said that they always trust their instincts, with 35 percent experiencing a corporal "gut feeling" having to do with situations.[20]

Without question, I see instinct as one of the greatest gifts we're born with. Think of it as a helping verb when you're getting ready to conjugate. It fits like a glove because one size fits all. I don't know, though, in which body part it resides. Our hearts, our minds, our goiters. No clue. Because it's an intangible, I don't assume it resides anywhere. I try not to define it at all, but I most certainly appreciate it, grateful for it being "there" every time I call upon it. Grateful it works, grateful it helps me even when I'm in a pissy mood.

Our instincts guide us. They keep us out of trouble and help with important decisions. They're like a built-in search engine when there's no Internet access. Instinct can't learn our lessons for us, though. That's cheating. I had always believed that my and everyone's instincts were infallible, but whenever I asked, "Can I trust so and so?" I had to learn on my own because, you guessed it, that's a lesson for me. Our instincts help; they don't do our work for us. Because of my past, or whatever, I may always have trust issues, but trying to learn that lesson alone keeps me quite busy and gives me something worthwhile to do. I'm grateful.

I've already told you how much I value alone time, something I'd never trade. An odd thing, though, is that whenever I use my instinct, I know I am not alone. Although I see it as a gift, it's more than that. It's like my instinct is a part of whoever or whatever made me in the first place. No, not my mother and father. It's bigger than that. I use the word God, and I use the pronoun "He" for Him. Feel free to select your own word or name or select nothing at all. This is the direction I go. My instinct kept me alive when I was a child, while I was growing into adulthood, and especially at age 34. Maybe it did the same for you as well. It probably always did and continues to do so. It seems to be there doing its thing without any prompting. But feel free to make use of it millions of times on demand. No matter how you stream it, it operates consistently every time and from any device.

Use it in moderation, though. When you need it most. Believe it or not, it works infallibly well when you have yes-no questions. One hundred percent right answers. There's a rather quirky method I've employed forever, something I've never told anyone about. I've never researched it because I just accept. There's no need to analyze. Just like when entering a Google query, I keep it simple and succinct. I never aim to confuse. Could be haphazard, could be whatever.

I'm very matter-of-fact. Whenever I ask a yes-no question (internally), where the answer is unknown to me, I receive it as a feeling on the left or right side of my head. Yes = left, right = no. No political associations are assigned here. Just the way it plays out. It's been this way for as long as I can remember. "Is my middle name Dean?" I just got a sensation on the left side of my head. It's unfair, though, because I already knew the correct answer. Now an unknown. "Is my car going to start this morning?"

Left-side. Great, no mechanic needed today. Sometimes, it elaborates with a condition, but most times, it does not. "Will I achieve such-and-such?" Left-side, "Yes, if you _____."

Sometimes, you get a no answer. And, trust me, you'll never ever get any response when the word "should" is present. "Should I lose weight?" No answer. No left, right, or center. Nothing. Up to you entirely. Your instinct doesn't tell you what to do. Nor should it. Oops. Another thing I've learned is that any query that references time (of any kind) works the same as should-questions. If you believe as I do, time doesn't exist in the spiritual world. When-questions are never recognized. They'd be invalid, untrue if received. Answers coming in regarding time wouldn't be coming from your instinct. They'd emanate from "wishful thinking" instead. Ain't no wisdom to be had there.

I'm grateful for the help I do receive. Grateful for my instinct. How about you? Do you value yours? Do you access it when you need it most?

Don't Plant Seeds in Old Soil

Out with the old, in with the new. For real. You're just about to wrap things up. Surrender past journeys. Every single one of them. Only a few words remain in the "What Now?" scheme of things, so sit up straight and let's hit it.

All those agendas that weren't yours to begin with, let 'em go. Same for all that advice others were spewing in your direction that you acted on. Erase it all. You know why? These outsiders may have had the best of intentions, but all visions came out through their lens, not yours. You're an individual. Be grateful for that. Only you know yourself better than anyone. You're now headed in a new direction, focused on your own lessons to learn via a new life to live, completely independent of stale, old inspiration.

Gratitude means being thankful for decades of your past (connections, friendships, relationships, situations, preparations, consolations, achievements, and accomplishments) that helped get you from where you began to where you are now. Damn, that's a lot of mileage. Be grateful for that wear and tear—it's the best part!

Bless all those people you've learned from. Now it's time to pick and choose, no longer accommodate merely because "it's easier." No time left for that nonsense. Now that you're prepping for the final stretch, the winner's circle known as "What's next?" you're gonna be so much quicker to let go of what no longer serves you and your best interests. See how fast you can do it. I'll start the timer now. Go!

I used to accommodate so much; it surprises me that my name's not Ramada Inn. Now, if I ever happen to tell my story, the complete version, and I hear back, "Well, pretend it never happened," I practice my language skills to see how many different ways I can say "goodbye." Very much related to when I'd told you how I feel about anyone who doesn't believe you or your story. They're invalidating you, undervaluing you, dismissing you and the totality of your life. Practice the following, and you'll be fluent in five languages: adiós, au revoir, arrivederci, auf Wiedersehen, and get lost.

Get ready for something else. When old friends, acquaintances, and family see that you're now focused on *your* lessons and witness your transformation, watch out! Instead of going all *When Harry Met Sally* by saying, "I'll have what she's having," they may instead try to steal from you. It takes courage to do your work, put in the effort, learn your lessons, and change (for the better). Bless those around you that are possibly too afraid to do it for themselves. Have compassion for them. It doesn't mean you halt your progress because of their fears, their agendas, and their possible jealousy. Bless them and let them go. You've got progress to make, and you'll never get to where you're going when your anchor's stuck to ~~the bottom of the sea~~ your past.

As you veer into the unknown and welcome it, please make sure to leave my stuff behind. *All* my stuff. All the lessons I've mentioned here that were mine may not be yours. I shared them to help you spark your vulnerability and recognize your uniqueness. Everyone's got their own stories, their own lessons; some shared, yet so very many universal. It just depends on where you are, which lessons you were born with, and how you've progressed thus far. Learning from a narcissistic mindset is a challenge, but I can't tell you how much I now value compassion as a result. On my own plateful of lessons, I've had patience, acceptance, empathy, standing up for myself, realizing I was "worth it," and knowing I could do all on my own. My own personal smorgasbord of lessons. Not necessarily a Happy Meal because I ain't a kid no more.

What's on your plate? I guarantee it: every time you attempt to tackle a lesson that's been put on your plate, you're never going to sing, "Plop, plop, fizz, fizz" again. Remember that commercial? Think it over; I'll give you time. All's going to go down so smoothly, no indigestion, no Rolaids needed. Savor all you've learned, especially the aftertaste. Those lessons learned and what you had to go through to learn them keep you from returning to the past. Oh, what a relief it is. Don't skimp either; a full plate reminds you you're here for a reason. You've got lessons. They're always fresh, and they never spoil. Pretty soon, you're going to order something new and not worry if you're going to like it or not. Bon Appétit and never feel uncomfortable when dining alone.

You and I aren't finished yet, but I must share something

with you now. I don't know when I began doing this, but whenever I chat or meet up with anyone, especially a stranger (in person, via Zoom, on the phone, by email, or text), I always express gratitude before parting, always. Sometimes, I preface the thanks with, "You just never know if you're ever going to see someone again." It's never a given. Sometimes, this catches the recipient by surprise, but to me, it's a necessity. Thank you.

You. Before I start singing "I'm So Glad We Had This Time Together" after I've done the Tarzan yell, I'm going to say thanks for sharing this time with me, for our meaningful exchanges. I see you on these pages, and I'm not making a joke. We all have lessons, and I know they're not easy to learn. More than anything, I hope you learn to welcome, accept, and appreciate lessons as much as I have. Learning them is the most lucrative investment you'll ever make.

All Living Things

Every day (in the bathtub), I do a little meditation, oftentimes referred to as Loving-Kindness Meditation. It's an easy and quite common one. I still don't know if I'm doing it right, but I find it effective. Its purpose: wishing everyone and all living things well. There's a chronology to it when wishing for others (after yourself):

1) Your teachers and mentors
2) Family, friends, and loved ones
3) Acquaintances/neutrals
4) The difficult ones
5) All living things.

That last wish (for all living things) is my favorite. The scripts may vary for this particular meditative training, but the essence remains the same. You know it? Perhaps you have practiced it already. If you're curious, please Google it; you may be glad you did. Good luck!

Two summers ago, near Lake Tahoe, there were massive and widespread wildfires. Thousands upon thousands of trees, acreage, and structures were destroyed. At the same time, so was the wildlife. Bears, bobcats, birds, coyotes, squirrels, mountain lions, deer, and more were killed or displaced. At that time, they needed warm wishes more than anyone. So, I gave them mine and threw in gratitude for good measure.

I will always be so grateful to my parents for giving me life and, more than that, for giving me a life to live: lessons. Big ones. I'd also be as grateful to them had they given me nothing, grateful to them for being exactly who they are, period. For the past twenty or so years, I had been more grateful for my life's purpose (my lessons) than I was for life itself. I knew I was here to learn lessons: an obligation, what needs to be done, the reason I'm here in the first place. But I wouldn't still be here at all had it not been for…

In the early-to-mid-nineties, I expected. Oops. I expected that—by accomplishing what I felt to be miracles by having solved the mystery of my past, the "reason for my unhappiness"— I would be rewarded for having come up with the truth. In Half Moon Bay, California, only a few weeks after I had moved there, a few months after I'd learned about the abuse and murder, a reality I never could have imagined, a visitor came to my bedroom door. Every day. A cat named Samantha.

When not at my door, I'd see her on the walking trail, coming up to me and others passing by. Samantha loved her audience, and she charmed them regularly. She was a neighbor cat belonging to someone down the street, as evidenced by the tag attached to her collar. But, one day at my back door, Samantha's behavior appeared different. She was panicky. I didn't know what was wrong. I chatted with her and petted her. This pattern of her being at my door repeated two more times that same day and night. What I finally noticed was that there was a sharp, pointy burr lodged inside her ear, and I couldn't pull it out. Although not my cat, I took her to a local vet and had it removed. Samantha was happy.

Soon after, Samantha came to my door again, this time with her collar stretched from her neck and leg. Ouch. I fixed this. This is when I put a blanket down on the spare bed and let her sleep on it at night, even though my lease prevented pets. Oops, again. I began feeding her and giving her attention and love. She didn't care that I had gained a hundred pounds overnight and was severely anxious around the people, the people, the people.

If you've got pets or had pets, be grateful! Big time! In many cases, they're way better than people. Unconditional love, no matter what.

Having Samantha around brought calm to my very chaotic mind at the time. I was on a mission. To expose the truth. To get it out. The injustice of it all. After telling others, journalists, and the authorities about what had happened, nothing happened. IMHO, keeping this murder a secret equals the crime of murder itself. If I wanted the truth to come out, I had to do it myself. I knew nothing at all about writing, but I was determined to write. I immersed myself in that world, took a host of creative writing classes, went to writers' conferences and conventions, belonged to writers' groups, started writing short stories, and eventually joined the Author's Guild. My narrative account of the discovery of my past was to be called SOUL*heresy* (later fictionalized and published as *The Seventh Ritual*). During that time, it was still customary to query literary agents and publishers on paper and submit through postal mail. Within a few months, every wall in that spare room where Samantha slept at night was covered with rejections.

I wasn't getting the rewards I felt I deserved. So much of my life was dismal, and I didn't see it getting any better. While still digesting the past I'd never known before, hope was disappearing. I ended up being offered my first writing job and was overjoyed until that gift disappeared as fast as it came. In reality, I more than likely didn't feel worthy; perhaps I sabotaged its manifestation. I was ecstatic about its offer, grateful to the people who offered it. For the longest time, I blamed them for taking it back. Oops. Wrong. I didn't know it at the time, but I only sought answers on the outside because I felt so powerless, empty, and unworthy inside.

After showing up at a party—given by these same people—where I was uninvited, thinking that I deserved to meet someone there who would help me become a published writer, I of course did not and made a fool of myself by having been there at all. I humiliated and rejected myself all at once. After walking home from that party, horribly and unbearably sad, devoid of all hope and feeling that my past would forever be my present, I chose to enter my condo's garage instead of going through its front door. There, I got inside my car, closed the garage door, turned on the ignition, and let the engine run. I was done. This continued for a long while, it seems, something I'd never done or thought about before. In my head, I had a checklist of reasons to hang around. There was only one. Samantha.

She'd chosen me. No matter what. Who would feed her, care for her, if I weren't around? Nope. Not gonna happen. My mother and father gave me life, and Samantha kept me in it. Grateful. The following day, my friend Cassie happened to come over, and we went for a walk along the shore. I told her nothing about the day prior. We ended up sitting in the sand quietly, looking out at a whale nearby, and then we spotted another, then another, and plenty more. Remarkably close to the shore, now about twenty in total. I'd never seen anything like that before. All those living things.

Immediately after the beach, Cassie and I went to a coffee place in town. As soon as we stepped in, I saw someone so familiar yet very much out of place. It was a therapist, Jonathan, from San Francisco, whom I had been going to during the time of the discovery of my past while I was still living in the City. What was he doing on the coast in Half Moon Bay? Thirty-plus miles from the City? Needless to say, I was in desperate need of help, and Jonathan helped me get it. I'm grateful. Grateful to him. Grateful to Cassie. Grateful for those whales. Grateful for those circumstances. One more time, grateful to Samantha.

Are you grateful for your life? To your parents for having given you life? For the lessons they delivered to you? I still believe wholeheartedly that the biggest lessons any of us receive come from our parents, birth or otherwise. They bring us into the world, but it may be something or someone else that keeps us there. More than not, a living thing. Animals have mastered unconditional love. Humans have not.

Samantha was with me and all my geographic moves for the next ten years. No matter what my mood was, how much fear I had going on during a particular day, or how much people triggered me, Samantha was by my side. Unconditionally. In 2001, here at Lake Tahoe, she'd become extremely ill and had remained that way for months; no vet could figure out what was wrong. A powerful winter storm was coming. A blizzard. She kept sitting near the door, in front of it, to go out then. Go out in the freezing snow!? How odd. She kept looking back at me. Staring. The electricity went out, and I put her blanket directly in front of the gas-lit fireplace, the only warmth there was. She liked that.

I knew what was going on. I knew what I had to do. Selfish

if I didn't. I didn't have four-wheel drive and called my very kind neighbor, Jim. The next snow-covered morning happened to be perfectly sunny. Jim drove Samantha and me to the vet. It was the last time I saw her. The vet put her to sleep. When she had been sitting near the door, she was saying goodbye. She was ready to go, and I knew she was unafraid. It was as natural an occurrence as being born. Subsequent research led me to find that animals do this routinely. They go off to die peacefully with no fear or drama. Seems like humans are the only animals that fear death.

After Samantha had died, I felt I was maybe now ready, too. But not before saying thanks in the most profound way possible. I stayed in life because of her. I had to create the biggest "thank you" I could imagine. Samantha deserved this. Had she not been in my life, I would have checked out. *Don't Be Afraid of Heaven* (that book written in those cemeteries) was a middle-grade novel, one I wrote for—and dedicated to—Samantha. One of the protagonists in it was a little Black girl named Samantha, because my Samantha was a black cat.

Whenever you feel gratitude for life, for what you've learned in it, for what it's been about, thank your parents, friends from the past, acquaintances of the present, and forever and always, all living beings. Whether your interactions contain conditions or not, be thankful to them each and every. And because of those you've known and learned from, strive to be grateful to all living things unconditionally.

TAKE ACTION: Part 1
Again, it isn't selfish to focus on yourself once more.
- *Whether associated with your life's purpose or not, what are you grateful for?*
- *Are you grateful for all the blessings you have? The*

blessings you've been given in life?
- *Think long and hard. Is there anything, right at this moment, that you take for granted?*
- *Is there something you happen to dismiss that someone else considers to be a huge blessing/attribute of yours?*

Please list your answers on paper and keep them next to you.

TAKE ACTION: Part 2
- *Do you believe you possess an instinct? An internal guide/companion?*
- *If so, do you make use of it? How?*
- *If not, what forms of help do you receive? Who/what provides it?*
- *Whether you believe in instinct, how are you grateful for the help you receive?*
- *Elaborate. Explain how you convey your gratitude.*

Ask yourself:

"What's next?"

9

HOPE

Hope never dies, but it certainly needs revival the closer we are to retirement. This chapter aims to jumpstart your hope by taking you back momentarily. To the time you felt the most hope ever. No harm in that. The pages here also teach you to be a gracious receiver and take hope from others who willingly share it. Discard what no longer serves you and unburden yourself from perpetual feelings of hopelessness.

It's out there. Plentiful. Available to everyone. All you learned thus far, the new life you've created for yourself via living your purpose, will be your solid foundation. Hope builds upon that. Gets you from A to B. At the end of this chapter, you will be asked to acknowledge the hope and the blessings you've received. You'll learn to value your instinct and the help it's given you.

Do you lead by example? Whether you realize it or not, people around you follow you. And not just on X (formerly Twitter). Just as you've been inspired by others, you do the same back. Everyone's story is worth hearing and deserves to be shared. We all learn from one another. The good, the bad, the ugly, and whatever is in between. Learning from others breeds hope inside us. Can hope be manufactured from within? It's sometimes too difficult. How can you possibly see the light when you're perpetually kept in the dark?

Who are your heroes? You must have some. And remember, you don't need to be a kid to have any. From the sports world? Military veterans? Titans of the business realm? Human rights advocates? Religious leaders? Spiritual gurus? Some superhero on film? A never-say-die champion in real life? Barrier-breaking pioneers? Or someone you know who has inspired you in a profound and long-lasting way?

Fiction or Fact?

Hopeful Harper became newly retired at seventy and spent nearly a year looking for what's next. Harper tried out new hobbies and sought out new friends but hit gold when encountering an old one, Purposeful Pat.

Pat, from Northern California's Silicon Valley, and Harper, from Birmingham, Alabama, both met at Stanford as undergrads decades earlier, went their separate ways upon graduation, and forged lives completely different from one another. Neither had communicated with the other in nearly fifty years.

In college, as one would imagine, Pat was filled with purpose and Harper with hope. Pat's ambition was off the charts, fulfilling all on an already full agenda until Pat retired. At 65, Pat sought more, a new way of doing things and a different and more satisfying way to live life. As usual, Pat got what Pat went after—a new life filled with the purpose of learning lessons, Pat's purpose for life, and Pat's *new* purpose. Fully unstuck from the old, Pat routinely sought out new adventures every day after retirement. One of those included a solo vacation to a destination never before visited, St. Lucia. Pat was more than excited to go and couldn't wait to learn a new lesson or master one of its repeats.

Harper's hope had been running thin. Harper had lived most of life as a dreamer, head in the clouds, living out an existence that had been programmed since birth by others. Change was in store. Hope keeps you going but only takes you so far. Harper's hope, stifled at a young age due to familial commitments, kept Harper stuck. Although graduating with an advanced degree in philosophy, Harper made little to no use of it. Harper's lifelong dream, stifled from the start, was to create an organization devoted to hope for humanity.

The family textile business occupied life full-time until a disability forced retirement. "What's next?" is a question that occupied Harper's mind until reservations were made, and off Harper went to the Caribbean Island of Barbados. A lone retreat with no family influences or obligations. Free, easy, and open-minded to all things new and different. Harper was raised by racist parents and, at seventy, was open to the notion of leaving outdated biases behind once and for all. Even post-retirement, Harper still felt an attachment to the racism embedded inside long ago, knowing full well how wrong it was. Living out another's destiny is living a false life. Better late than never.

Harper seldom flew internationally, and changing planes in Miami was a bit overwhelming until fate stepped in. The seat Harper had been assigned had been changed due to a mechanical malfunction. Harper's new location was a window seat, and Harper only liked the aisle. Harper's new neighbor must have known this when asking, "Would you like to switch?"

Before Harper could answer, the other passenger said, "I know you," before saying, "I'm Pat."

After a bit of back and forth, the two reconnected as if no

time had passed at all. Harper spoke of life in the South, and Pat, life in the West. Pat was comfortable sharing personal stories, while Harper remained guarded. Because of this, Pat talked, and Harper listened. This lasted the full three and a half hours from Miami to Barbados.

Pat spoke of forced retirement and the lessons it brings. Overwhelmingly, Pat spoke of what life had been like after putting Pat first. No longer living for others, their agenda(s), no longer pleasing, and more. "You were always so hopeful," Pat said.

"Yes, I guess I was. Back then."

"It'll come back to you in Barbados. I'm sure of it. That's when change happens, when your guard's down. On vacation."

Harper nodded. "Wouldn't that be nice? I hope."

After the two landed, before they left each other's company, Harper thanked Pat for those stories shared. Pat thanked Harper for listening, then said, "Remember, there's a lesson out there waiting for you." They departed the plane; Pat went on to the connecting flight, and Harper to the arrival area.

Harper enjoyed what the trip had to offer and, on the second to the last day, chose to drive around the island. Though Harper was initially intimidated by the steering wheel being on the right side of the car, Harper began to enjoy the scenery. From the main town of Bridgetown, up to Speightstown on the west shore to the North Point, then down the east to Mount Gay and St. Nicholas Abbey (a must-see sight on TripAdvisor), a former plantation house. Harper had known of many in the southern United States but had never visited one before.

When Harper arrived, no other tourist was there. It was after hours and off-season. Harper was keen to at least peek in. "We're closed now, but I can show you around, if you like," a younger male guide offered.

Not there more than a few minutes, Harper was shown the

insides of the defunct plantation's administrative office. An accounting ledger from 1831 was on display in the entry area and propped up at an angle to be viewed by those interested. Harper admired the vintage penmanship, then asked, "What's this? Atlas? Worth five dollars."

"Atlas. A horse, stallion."

"A horse is listed as an asset?"

"Oh, yes. Definitely."

"What about this one? Old Jake. Zero."

"He was a slave."

"Zero? But the horse. Five dollars."

"Slaves had no value. Especially the old ones."

This exchange, this story, this divulgence, this living and visible proof on paper that transmuted into a personal message lasted with Harper for the remainder of the trip. A tangible lesson that's never to be forgotten. Any person valued at zero (by anyone else) was more than Harper's preconceptions would allow. Wrong. Horribly wrong. A bit of hope re-entered Harper's being and aligned with Harper's desire for justice. Hopeful Harper was inspired by Pat, shaken to the core by that ledger, and motivated to make sure that another Old Jake would never again be designated as an asset or liability.

Harper's dream, Harper's hope for humanity, was re-born in Barbados because of a life-changing event, its aftermath, and the recognition of the lessons of a lifetime that follow.

So, back to you. Who'd you come up with? Your hero? Who is it? Chances are they made you feel hopeful in your own life. Be thankful for that person.

Hope does keep us going. For sure. A study by the Human Flourishing Program at Harvard University's Institute for Quantitative Social Science found that hope is vital to senior mental health. Fostering hope as you age also decreases the risk of developing mental health indicators like anxiety and depression.[21] *The Oxford Handbook of Hope* 2017 publication *Promoting Health in Older Adults* also mentions that the happiest, most optimistic older adults rejected the standard stereotypes about aging. Exercising more, finding a higher purpose, and joining a senior day program or group, are also mentioned as ways of manufacturing and maintaining hope.[22]

    If you can muster hope without expectation, you just hit the jackpot. When you were younger, could you disassociate one from the other? Or were they intertwined? That's all you knew to do then because of your youthful naïveté. You didn't know at the time that learning lessons was your purpose in life. If you could go back, you'd tell younger (your name here), "Duh!"

    All duhs aside, go back with me for a bit and think of your younger self as we travel together. No, not to the past, really, because I told you, we're done with that. Let me share with you the time in my life when I felt the most hope. It was all over the place. That's all I could feel when only optimism was before me.

    Picture it: an era away from retirement. San Francisco. 1979. I was 21, had just moved to the City, and was close to graduating from the University of California, Berkeley. My whole life was ahead of me. I felt I could have anyone and make anything happen. I wanted to be a working actor, have my own sitcom, and be in a relationship. At 21, hopes and dreams consumed my mind. Same for you, too? It's easy to recall that feeling because it was just too good.

    As you read, in the back of your mind, continue to take your own journey backward to hopefulness. In the front of your mind, please stay with me. Now, jump ahead a few decades to the here and now, but keep remembering that time of your life when you had nothing *but* hope. Don't leave any details out. Your hopes, dreams, and more. Remember that feeling—*hope*—and discard everything else attached to it (circumstances, age, and expectations). Just the feeling. Like your life is just beginning. That all things are possible. Hold onto it, and don't let it go. Bring it with you because the journey's not over. It's just beginning.

Now, the rest of the equation. Were you good at math in school? It doesn't matter. You're an adult now. Fake it 'til you make it. Hope + _____ = a successful, fulfilling life. Find the missing element. What's that element? Anyone? Anyone? Bueller? Anyone? The correct answer is wisdom. And how do you get that? Lessons learned, that's how. No other integer completes the equation successfully. When you combine hope with wisdom, you've got the world by the balls. You've mastered it and them. When you were younger, you may have thought you had it all. You fool. Having it all is not available to you 'til you're older. Sometimes, not even then. It depends on how you define "all," and even after that, it takes work.

School teaches us a lot of things. At Berkeley, before dosing off in my Paleontology 101 class, I learned that "coprolites" is the word for dinosaur poop. Yes, I learned an impressive body of knowledge while there, but it didn't make me any wiser. Most if not all wisdom is acquired in life, not school. UC Berkeley created memories for me, but it's the hope I had back then I want to remember most, so I can take it with me now.

A lot of that hopeful kid still lives inside me. But at this point, during retirement, I have to dig deeper to find him, remember him. Do you have a kid living inside you? A hopeful kid? Do some digging. That kid inside you, filled to the top with hope, is just dying to be re-discovered.

Classic sitcoms still remind me of hope, of all the years and experiences to come. What do you watch? Do you still play? Do you play the fool? It's much different than being one. Playing gets you out of your head and gives your mind a break in between lessons. Hope's not easy to muster sometimes, but if you can (somehow) make it to midnight, a new day comes along within mere seconds. Hope begins again. It's in your hands. If it slipped out, ask your younger you to pick it up. It's there somewhere. Enjoy your time looking. And, while we're waiting for you (*and* Ferris Bueller), a joke I loved telling as a kid: What's the stinkiest show on TV? Gomer's Pyle.

Life's Purpose Is Never-Ending

One more time! Lessons (aka life's purpose) last until the day you die. If they didn't, you'd already be gone.

Right now, just like you sought out your most hope-filled stint in life, reflect one more time on your life-changing event and its aftermath. And don't hang out too long there. Just a brief visit to remind you of the time when your life changed forever in the biggest way imaginable. Details aren't important here, just the realization that this is when your life truly began. The time when your truth hits you smack in the face every time you look into the mirror immediately after waking up in the morning. There it is. It's the best you that you're ever going to see. Except for the aftermath of flossing your teeth and discovering what's left there on the string. Gross.

After that life-changing event, reflect on all you've learned. From all those lessons and all that weren't. All those years of knowledge gained and wisdom acquired. Look at how far you've come. You could fill a book, for sure. If curious, ask yourself:

- What's the biggest lesson that remains?
- How far have I come while learning it?
- Is this *the* lesson of my life? Why I'm here?
- What was the biggest lesson I've learned completely (thus

far)?
- Is it complete? Or is there more to learn?
- Have repeat lessons of long ago vanished?
- Am I less surprised when lessons appear and when?
- Do any of them surprise me at this point?
- When a lesson appears now, do I accept it for what it is? Am I grateful for it?
- Has all this wisdom acquired given me hope?

Hope means different things to different people. It's not necessarily synonymous with optimism, expectation, or optimistic expectation. It's a feeling exactly the same as all others but unique. As mentioned earlier, I still believe that it's impossible to manufacture hope from within, or it's extremely difficult to do so. That's why it's vital to look outside yourself. Get out of your head. Be open to being inspired by others.

Here's a standout. Harvey Milk is a hero to many and should never be forgotten. He instilled hope by example. Milk was one of the first openly gay elected officials in the United States. At a time when most were in, he was out. Harvey Milk lived the truth every day when others felt they couldn't. He gave hope to thousands who called the closet their home.

A few months after I'd moved to San Francisco—that time of my life when I'd felt the most hopeful—an event occurred there that's called the White Night riots (May 1979). It seemed like the entirety of San Francisco was under siege because of outrage and injustice. In 1978, a San Francisco City Supervisor shot and killed Mayor George Moscone and Supervisor Harvey Milk. In 1979, Dan White—charged with murder—was convicted of voluntary manslaughter and received a much-reduced sentence of seven years in prison vs. life. The verdict and its violent and chaotic aftermath changed the way I view San Francisco. Senseless deaths should never go unnoticed. Moscone and Milk shaped a city that fostered acceptance, liberty, and hope. They should be remembered for this and for so much more.

Decades after having lived there, I see San Francisco as a city of hope. It still delivers hope to thousands. When I left there in 1992, I thought homophobia had become extinct, and liberty for all was a done deal. Three decades later, both are still works in progress. I hope.

Who has inspired you? Is there someone you look up to? Have looked up to? Is there a place that makes you feel hope more than another? Just as others give us hope, just as we inspire others by our own examples, sometimes it's an intangible that lifts our spirits and makes us want to soar. Where's yours? Sometimes it's where you live, where you used to live, sometimes it's a place you've visited while on vacation or had seen on TV. Nature? Where exactly? Unadorned, as is, simple, unpretentious, anything that's the opposite of man-made. Locate that certain spot that breeds hope and go there inside your mind.

It's worth repeating that time's more precious now. With all the tools we've assembled along the way, why not make use of any hope we've collected and use it as frequently as possible? It doesn't come at a price, but finding it can't be done for us. It's our responsibility to seek it out, to notice when others are handing it out freely, and to appreciate them for having done so. And spread it around; lead by example; inspire others. Share your story, your lessons, and how you learned them, and describe their value and importance. Give hope to others. You'll be glad you did.

A New Day

At the end of your working life, after you absorb all that you've learned and how far you've come, know that your next day begins anew. A fresh start. The chance to begin again. When a person first wakes up, they don't wake up ruminating. Dreams and nightmares may have entered your sleep, but the moment you awaken, you're fully in reality. The same one you were in yesterday, but with a new perspective. Your old perspective carries over from the previous day only if you allow it to. Instead, replace all with hope. Try meditating or deep breathing right off the bat, even if it only lasts a few minutes. Nothing complicated, only a natural calmness to start your day off. You no longer have deadlines to meet and no obligatory tasks to complete. You're the boss of your new life. When your alarm clock goes off in the morning, ease into your day with a relaxed approach that only retirement affords. A luxury, a gift, and a grand opportunity to master what's most meaningful.

It's common knowledge that folks coming from abusive childhoods veer towards control in adulthood more than others. Being a chronic controller is as incurable as living amongst the chaos. Balance is the key to a happier medium here. And never confuse control for order. When you live in an environment with minimal clutter and distractions, those answers come to you much more clearly. I'm not just talking about mess either—clothes on the floor, paperwork all over your desk. I'm also talking about too much time spent watching the news, too much interaction on social media, etc.—ways you're inviting chaos into your life. This is all clutter and mess. A distraction to you living a peaceful life with minimal obstruction.

A lot of folks aged 65 and over focus on relaxation techniques in order to sleep better: warm baths, meditation, herbal teas, shutting off all devices, and no TV.[23] But what about your surroundings? The environment you're going to enter the next day? When you've prepared it, when you've created order without going overboard, that is what you wake up to. You face less chaos. There's always going to be surprises. Whenever you invest in creating a peaceful environment to wake up to, your reaction follows suit. You wake up to less stress, less that must be done, fewer distractions. Mornings are the time of day you'll feel the most hopeful. You'll have the most positive energy before life intervenes.

How does your day begin? How's your energy in the morning?

Do you miss your job? The work you'd done? Your co-workers? Accomplishing? Multitasking? Are you discouraged because life's not what it once was? Do you look forward to waking up and beginning anew? Or do you dread it? All the greatness your new day presents begins with how your mind greets it.

The clearer your mind is, the easier it is to accept and even welcome the lessons you've got on your plate for that day. When your environment and your mind are chaos-filled, lessons, especially those new ones that enter your day that you weren't expecting, become stressful. The arrival of lessons is something we cannot control. The environment in which they're delivered can be, to a certain extent.

New days come to us systematically. And we can most value them when we view them one at a time. I am not so sure who invented daily planners, but keeping them jampacked = the same chaos as a closet filled with junk. Make it balanced, and account for the healthiest ingredient: improvisation. Wiggle room. Thinking and acting on the spot is not a bad thing at all. Having everything planned out is good organization, but it also means spending all that time prior ruminating, perhaps stressing over an activity that is to be. What's good about that? When you improvise every once in a while, you spend no time stressing over the activity beforehand, all because you didn't know about it.

My mind keeps taking me back to "bilanciata." The Italian

way of life. They work to live, not live to work. They also seem to laugh a lot. How about if you begin your own day with a laugh? When looking in the mirror, have a good belly laugh and watch your body shake. There's a lot of comedy going on there. All those mistakes made. Being different from others. It's funny. All those folks who don't "get you." Who cares! Laugh about it. When I lived in Italy, I used to go to WeightWatchers. In those days, journaling (our food diaries on paper) was obligatory. We had to enter everything we ate, and we had to turn our journals in to the leader before each meeting. Oops. I liked everyone there, especially the leader. Even when she read my journal to the entire room (in Italian) aloud.

"Frutti di mare?!? Per colazione?!?"

"*Yes*, a shrimp omelet. For breakfast."

The entire room erupted in laughter. I must have been in a good mood because I wasn't defensive that day. I laughed instead. I spent a bit of time explaining to the room that Americans may eat shrimp omelets, but there's no way I could convince a roomful of Italians that eating seafood for breakfast was acceptable. I went to that meeting for months and was ribbed about my shrimp omelets for just as long. Months' worth of laughs at my expense. Or was it? Depends on how you look at it. Not costly to me because I was laughing (at myself) just as hard. If you're up for a good laugh in Italy, try asking your restaurant server for parmesan cheese to put on your seafood pasta. How do you say "faux pas" in Italian? I won't give away what's going to happen to you next. A new day, a new way to see yourself, your life in a new, gentler light.

Hope comes from light. A positive attitude. Optimism. If you just cannot come up with it on your own, borrow it from elsewhere. It's out there all over the place. A bunch of people living brand new days. Hit up your neighbor first thing. Instead of just nodding when you see each other outside, say "Good morning" and see what happens. You may brighten up two lives at once by having done so. There's nothing better than a hope-filled start. It wasn't in your calendar; had it been, you'd have to think about it first and perhaps elect not to do it when the time comes. Extra points for acting spontaneously. Points that pay dividends.

Personal points (accomplishments) equal professional. If opening up to others is a lesson for you, you're living your life purpose by letting them in. Learn by taking unplanned action. Go with the flow vs. channeling it.

A Hopeful Recap

At this point in your life's journey, do you now see how your lessons are connected to your life's purpose? Do you have a better understanding of true purpose? Do you have a better understanding of its meaning? Importance? Don't you just love yes-no questions? No need to answer that one.

Hope means being unafraid of the future. Surprises are going to happen no matter what. There's no reason to fear an unknown tomorrow because it's always going to be unknown. Rumination: "Am I going to have gas tomorrow because of having eaten broccoli the night before?" Who the hell cares?!

One thing at a time. And when you do things one thing at a time, rather than trying to do them all at once, you're allowing hope to enter the picture, to squirm in there somewhere. Remember, the clearer moments you have, the more you're going to be able to see hope vs. dismissing it. Hope probably pays more visits than you realize. It's all up to you. When you see it first thing in the morning, snatch it up and don't let it go. Grasp onto it before your brain gets in the way and destroys it.

You know how you use Disk Cleanup on your computer? Right before you de-fragment your drives? Disk Cleanup is a way of cleaning out and cleaning up memory and storage on your computer so it will all run more smoothly. A tech housecleaning of sorts. Memory and storage. It's on your phone, your laptop, your desktop; it's everywhere and has its limits. Every device can handle only so much memory and storage. And don't say that's what clouds are for. If I wanted advice about clouds, I'd consult Al Roker. Sorry to snap.

What takes up the most space in your own personal drive (your brain)? If "regret" or "fear" place prominently on your bar graph, it's time for data cleansing. Time to replace the old with new. Un-learn and trade up. Did I mention that un-learning is a lesson? No one was born with fear; we learned it all. On most occasions, for survival. The thing is, if you're around my age, it's ludicrous to think that you still need that survival-fear you'd picked up during immaturity. It's more dangerous the longer it exists. Nothing kills hope more than a past that's masquerading as your present. Let it go once and for all. Don't hang onto fear just because it's all you know. A hopeful life is right on the other side of it.

Do you have allies in your life? Ally, singular? Allies share hope. They make you feel hopeful because you're never going it alone. Great if you do. If so, be grateful and make sure to say thanks. I had one all along and didn't even know it. Remember when I was talking about Aunt Shirley? A character in those middle-grade novels I used to write? Well, that was a real person. *My* Aunt Shirley. I used her name in those novels as a tribute. To thank her, in the same way I thanked my cat, Samantha. There's no way I could let my Aunt Shirley go unnoticed, unremembered. My Aunt Shirley wasn't a spiritual sage like the character, but she was the world's *best* storyteller. Always the perfect beginning, middle, and end to every tale told. And they were always funny.

A coincidence that the discovery of my life-changing event was happening at a time when my aunt was quite ill. As I was learning about the truth of my past, I had also come to feel that my aunt may have also known (about it). I suffered by not knowing. Had my Aunt Shirley known, perhaps she suffered by not having divulged this secret. My mother and father suffered for a host of reasons. Everyone suffers. Personal suffering is universal.

In the spring of 1992, after picking up my aunt from the East Bay and driving her to Half Moon Bay—where I was to move—I was en route to show my aunt some love and express eternal gratitude to her. No details, no past, no specifics were ever mentioned. More than anything, if my aunt had ever felt regret of any sort, I wanted it to be gone. She and I were seated at a window table at a coast side restaurant, and other than each other, all we could see was the Pacific Ocean. After my words, Aunt Shirley was gazing out at the water. I was gazing at both. A few weeks later, she died.

She was not buried in the East Bay, where she had been living. Instead, she was buried in San Bruno (facing the bay), rather close to me on the same peninsula as Half Moon Bay (facing the ocean), my new home then. I'd drive over to see her many times at the cemetery. I'd do all the talking, and Aunt Shirley couldn't answer back or tell me to shut up.

This happened for months, years, even after I moved away from the area. In mid-1992, I was so afraid of living this newly-discovered, truth-filled life. Terrified. I relied on my aunt for comfort even though she was long gone. I kept going until, one day, I was prohibited from visiting. They were doing plumbing work and re-paving the road to where my aunt was buried. At the entrance, I met a woman who told me that her loved ones didn't want her to visit anymore. She had had a car accident driving to the cemetery, and her car was totaled her last time there. I knew I was meeting this woman for a reason. I truly felt her grief.

More than not, you hear stories for a reason. I felt hers was mine. Aunt Shirley didn't want me to visit her anymore. Maybe she never did in the first place. In my mind, I pictured her saying, "Get lost! Stop coming here! Move on!" Such a real image to me. Not angry. Firm. "Start living life vs. tolerating it! Get on with it! Bury the past!" See, she always ends with humor.

I didn't visit her again, except once by accident, when her husband, my uncle, ended up being buried next to her several decades later. I saw his name on one side of the headstone, my aunt's (and their infant son's) on the other. For the past several decades, I have had dreams with so many of the same people making repeat appearances. Including Samantha. *Many* times. Thirty-one years have passed since my aunt's death, and I've never had one dream with her in it. Hard to believe, easy to understand. Abstractly connected to my surreal past, I can only speculate that my aunt stays away so I can move on, not being further reminded of anything that's not the present. I'll accept that. I'm grateful for that. I'm always grateful to her. I'm even grateful for my past and to be in the present alongside the presence of hope.

Are you seeing more hope in your life now? Even a little bit? If so, be grateful for it. If not, be grateful for something else you've got. By doing so, you're opening yourself up to the arrival of _____. Gratitude opens doors. Maybe hope's behind it.

What a Journey!

So, how'd you get from there to here? Now, that's a loaded question. Don't focus on the details (of the whole thing) because no one's going to get it anyway. Life's about the gist of things.

When you're a senior, who has the time to wait for someone else to figure you out? Hope means letting go of how others see you and what they think of you and your agenda (whether you've got one or not).

Having lots in common is fantastic, but seriously, know for a fact that you've learned more from others you'd *assumed* you had little in common with. Assuming is a huge mistake. Not everyone's book cover mirrors the story they keep inside. Hope also means learning all you can learn from old stories, old lessons. Then, let them go. No extra credit is given for writing an essay about "My Life: The Early Years" when it's already been told a million times over. Enough already. Know when it's time to move on and let go. Hope builds when you have told your story so many times that it would literally make you sick to have to tell it again. And, again, don't bother telling it to anyone because you want them to see or acknowledge the real you. With the popularity and reliance upon social media, superficiality has overtaken the real world anyway.

When you meet someone, and they ask you to please like, comment, share, or subscribe, go OG instead. On a nature walk, say to a stranger, "Beautiful day, isn't it?" Maybe they were having a really tough day, and you didn't know it when you spoke to them. Maybe it was you who was having the bad day. Yes, sounds shallow, but more times than not, those words may yield something either one of you is meant to hear or exchange. You never know 'til you get those words or gestures out.

Forbes magazine often publishes articles exclusive to retirees. One from 2019 ("Why It's Important To Stay Social In Retirement And How To Do It" by Rob Pascale) emphasizes the importance of senior bonding. Any interaction counts. The article cites that staying socially connected is essential to one's well-being. It provides a sense of belonging, feeds individual identity, adds value to life, enhances self-worth, and keeps levels of stress in check.[24]

With motives, expectations, and agendas (aka people-pleasing) aside, maybe those simple words alone will foster hope. Hope for a beautiful day—even if it may not be—just because you said it was. It could turn the other person's day around. Or your own.

In my 20s and early 30s, I had many friends. I socialized constantly. Didn't believe in lessons then or much of anything else, but I do recall these friends asking me for advice on occasion. Something I noticed then still applies. Female and male friends, straight and gay, used to ask, "Clint, what's the best way for me to meet someone?" Easy answer. "Go on vacation. Happens every time." When you're meeting someone while on a journey to a vacation destination, the other person is going to be in the same boat as you. Away from their agendas, schedules, imposed or self-imposed routines. Vacations breed hope. Two people experiencing the same thing, free from tired, old restrictions, being open and vulnerable, seeing what's out there. What could be better than two people on their own individual journeys feeling nothing but the new together?

Keep selfies to a minimum while there. Not that I ever did, but I stopped taking them once I realized that my double chin had multiplied. Save those turkey necks for Thanksgiving dinner. It's all about the new and different now. How exciting is that? Are you with me? Your new journey only begins when you've put those old ones to rest. Re-visits are nice but aim to throw in something that's not the same old, same old. Discover new paths, and don't Google their conclusions beforehand. Instead, find out for yourself via your own feet on the ground.

Put the past to rest once and for all. Place it in the bin and permanently delete it. Like a butterfly, it transformed you. It got you from A to B, and you're the one that filled all that in between with wisdom. The icing on the cake. Yum if it's got dark chocolate in it. I always tell myself that dark chocolate's healthy, so it's OK to eat. It is, isn't it?

Pretty soon, I'm going to give you an acting exercise that'll hopefully become your own reality show: *Play the Fool!* You're perfectly cast for the part. Before your audition, though, you gotta discard that old script and shred it. It's outdated, and the pages have been rewritten several times over. Some are even illegible by now. Naturally, spontaneity's a plus; Diane Chambers and Monica Geller, thanks so much for coming. Don't call us, we'll call you.

Over the Hump

There's a purpose in doing, after all. A big one. Remember when we discussed that life's purpose is all about learning (lessons) and has little or nothing to do with doing, achieving, or accomplishing? Of course you do because that's been repeated about a million times already. Doing builds momentum. Gets you unstuck. Helps move you along from nowhere to somewhere. Even if you do a little, you can say after, "I did it. I did something." A huge victory for some aiming to get off the hump. Even if you experience little to no despair and depression in life, keep doing when you least want to. Especially if there's something you *have* to do.

As a new retiree, you're still in the game. You did it. Whether it's too much of a stretch or not, you've set off hope. It doesn't take much. There are times that come about when your mind tells you, "No. Not gonna happen. Never gonna happen. What are you thinking?!" That's nothing but fear talking. Rather than telling your mind to take a hike, take a risk instead. Even better, take action. Do anything. Any task or undertaking. Make the effort. Any movement forward equals more than just thinking about doing. That little feat becomes *huge* because you defied your negative mind. How your mind ever got that way no longer matters; it's your past that's now been kicked to the curb. Good riddance.

The seriousness of depression should never be minimized, nor what it takes to treat it. Any advice, suggestion, or anecdote offered on a page will never be a sufficient substitute for what a professional is able to do for you. Not even close. Your life experience is unique, but sharing does bring us together. In a lot of cases, it makes us feel less alone. It brings out the human in us. Rip off and discard that cover so we can get to the meat of your story.

When I first started researching details about writing this, my first non-fiction book, I found something helpful and interesting. "Make sure your personal is universal…or don't include it." I hope so much you find relevancy in the anecdotes I've shared with you.

Sometimes, I can think of nothing to write at all. Are there times you stall? Can't think of what to include next? You're not alone. Often, the delay lasts for a few seconds or hours or maybe even days or weeks. You're ready when you're ready. When your mind's most clear is when your light usually turns green.

Whether a camel or not, humps exist for everyone. You're not alone.

No matter how you get there, I hope that hope finds you when you need it most, by any means. In the meantime, let in the notion that you're about to let go and have some fun. Get ready for a deep exhale. Get ready to enjoy life!

TAKE ACTION
- *Look back for the last time; let go of any focus on the past. You've done and learned enough for the moment.*
- *Feel free to erase all previous writing and delete any files you've created...or not.*
- *But, right now, erase all from your mind and look back no more.*
- *You're living your purpose; you've learned your lessons and will continue to do so.*
- *Lessons will be coming to you until the day you die, so in the meantime, pat yourself on the back as you face forward.*
- *Get excited!*

10

SUCCESS

As a new retiree with a fresh foundation securely in place, all that's left is the good stuff. You know your life purpose because you've identified it via the aftermath of your life-changing event. You're living the truth as you recognize your repeat lessons while making your way through life simply as is. You accept any and all that your life's about, and you're grateful for it. You've rediscovered the hope you once had and integrated it into your new life. You're living life as it was meant to be lived, and now, finally, it's your turn to pick and choose the way it turns out. Success.

Continuing to ask "why?" keeps you going. It keeps you and your true purpose alive. It adds meaning and value to a life already worth living. You've completed all prerequisites, and now it's time for the electives. Choose wisely (or don't). Nearing the end of this chapter, you'll be asked to create and maintain your to-do list. Become enthusiastic about things you've never done before. More than anything, you'll be asked to demonstrate your wisdom now that you're a wise, old(er) soul.

Be wise, have fun, and get ready to enjoy the best time of your life.

You are so there. Living life. Learning lessons is nothing new to you. You've been doing it all these years, but now you've moved it up a notch. Instead of a footnote, you now realize lessons are your text block, your purpose for living the life you've been given. When you know you're living your purpose, you reinforce the common knowledge that you're as vital as you've ever been. You continue to work towards a goal, just as hard (or not) as you ever have. Never a race, no competitors or runners-up. Lessons don't discriminate, and everyone's got them.

It all should be such a given by now. Remember those? Givens? You've always learned from life as you've made your way through it, but now you should know that lessons mean more. As seniors, they're weightier than before. And no better feeling than the moment they're learned. Lessons learned make you feel productive, build esteem, and create a stronger, more forceful you. They're as worthwhile as you are. For the most part, lessons seem to arrive when they're supposed to, into a world where perfect timing doesn't exist. Awesome that breaks and breathers arrive in between, mini vacations that turn into bigger ones once you realize a lesson is coming because they always do. Freaking out when they arrive is also an option, but best to leave all that to the drama queens. Tiaras optional.

You've earned so much by getting to this point. If you've spent too much of your life existing via your survival brain (your left side), give your right equal time. By coming this far, surviving is a given. You're doing it. You've got it down. So now, ease up and see what else is new by playing the fool. Newness keeps you on your toes, keeps you fresh, and reignites enthusiasm for all that's turned stale. As far as you can recall, have you ever entered "learn lessons" into your daily planner? Probably not. It's engrained. Goes without saying. It's an actionable item every day that requires no "do-by" date.

And it's a general rule of thumb that repeat lessons aren't as desirable. Duh. More time devoted to the same, old, same old? No, thank you. Learn as you go along and insist on balance. If you feel you haven't been given a break in between lessons, create one for yourself. You've earned it. Nourish your right brain that's ravenous, eager to dream and be creative. Go on vacation inside your mind. Allow yourself to be free there, as free as you want to be. Some folks were born this way, some not. Some were raised with balance; survival (left) brain = 50 percent, creative (right) brain = 50 percent. That's easy math that even I can understand. Harvard Health Publishing has printed research studies of brain laterality and concluded that no evidence of "sidedness" exists. The statistics of thinking "right brain" vs. "left brain" lack proof that "sidedness" is either fact or myth.[25] Instead of university findings, you be the judge. Research studies are scientific and need proof to be valid. Are lessons and their relation to your life's purpose real? Or not? Calculate for yourself.

Whatever ratio you've got going on right now, mix it up. You're good. Your true purpose has been identified. You have a much better idea as to why you're here. Always be proud of the life your left and right brains have created for yourself and your family. It took a lot of doing that will never be overlooked or forgotten. Those noble accomplishments will be with you forever and last as long as your learned lessons. They could be of equal measure. Look at all the good you've got going on, all you were born with, all you've made happen, all you've collected, all you've learned. It's all good.

In your working life, success was perhaps measured by profitability. In retirement, there's more to it than just that. Do you still measure your own personal success by external factors? Internal? Or a mix of both? Success is a subjective experience.

Measure yours by your own standards and values. As a senior individual, it makes sense that the greatest measure of success is depth. How deep is your well? Not your well of knowledge but your well of wisdom. It takes decades to fill that one. I hope yours is full. If yours is nearing its brim, voilà. Immeasurable success.

By this point, you've answered all those why questions. You know why you chose the path you did, why this and that happened, why you've lived the life you've lived, and why you've lived it this precise way. So many choices you've made, some choices made for you. You've learned so much, and you've grown wiser. A great place to be. Now for some more white space. Let a few blank spots stay that way. No need to fill up each and every one.

And let's get clear: surrender doesn't mean giving up. It means taking the pressure off yourself once in a while. Let some things happen vs. feeling like you have to *make* them happen. Forcing things too much usually forces a lesson. Gotta love those lessons, but let's not get crazy. Tackling too many at once will make you that way. Accept and be grateful for your time off. Accept and be grateful for what fun means to you. This means different things to different people. If others yawn at your unique version of fun, let 'em. They could be tired and need a nap. Don't ever feel the need to define it at all. Think nature, with someone or alone (when needed), on a sunny day when all's quiet, peaceful, calm. It could be the time of your life if you let it, especially when you add newness to it, when you allow it to happen on its own and don't know where you're going to end up. An adventure that leads you to marvel is one I highly recommend.

Marvel at the unknown. There's tons of that out there. Tons. Marvel when something good happens that you weren't expecting. Marvel when good elevates to great. It's hard to know for sure what exactly keeps a person young, but marveling has got to be up there somewhere. You always deserve good things. Tons of things only happen when you make them happen. The rest happens as it happens. Marvel at all. Marvel at the not knowing. Ask a lot of questions because you always want to be smarter today than you were yesterday. When you don't ask, don't tell, nothing happens. You don't learn a thing.

Question when you're hungry, appreciate when you're full. I don't know if there's a real Clean-Plate Club. There probably is somewhere.

Walk with Me

Hey, thanks for joining me here today. Glad to see you. You've got your walking shoes on. That's a good move; some parts are a bit tougher than the rest. Have you ever been here before? Looks like this might be your first time. Well, as you know, this is by far the best experience I've ever known in life—walking in nature—and I'm so grateful for your company right now.

Spooner Lake. A bit to the east of Lake Tahoe. Northern Nevada. Still don't know why it's called that; there's a plaque I've seen somewhere around here that explains the name, but I've already forgotten what it says. You like what you see? The pine trees? The lake? The snowflowers in bloom? The silence? Those moments of soft sounds? Nice, ain't it? A flat walk, with little change in elevation. That's why I like walking vs. hiking. Keep it simple. Keep everything simple and appreciate the hell out of the simplicity.

That gravel mashing into the dirt as we step over it. Listen. Evidence that you're doing something. Evidence that you're experiencing nature vs. just watching it on TV. Look. Your socks are already getting dirty. Doesn't matter. More evidence. Look at that bird hovering near that treetop. And that couple gazing at it with binoculars. I think I overheard them talking once before; one describing to the others what kind of bird that is, but I forgot that part, too. Not so important. Again, relish the experience, not how it's defined. Feel that barely warm breeze that just came up. An indication that spring has ended, but summer hasn't yet begun. Some snow still on the ground in places where the sun doesn't shine. A reminder of what was, what's still left.

All created, not one thing man-made. Well, except for those plaques and a few benches. At least they're painted in earth tones. That works. Are you enjoying this? We'll stop if you get winded; the air's thinner up here. Different from Tahoe, isn't it? All the tourists go there, yet none ever seem to come here. Nice to have the option of going to either. Nature's everywhere. A wonderful day to be had whenever you're near it, a privilege to actually experience it firsthand. Don'tcha think? There's a bench coming up soon if you're tired. I used to remember the names of the folks they're dedicated to, the names on the benches. They'll come to me once we get closer.

Last fall, a hiker told me that there were two bears ahead, higher up the mountain. By the time I got there, I could barely see them. They snapped pictures. I don't really like to do that. I let things be. Let those bears have just as much peace as we're enjoying. Glance, but don't gawk. How rude. I'm not one for dinner parties, so here is where I show my best manners. This is where they count most. This is where your words, your thoughts, the way you react to things, and your expressions of gratitude are observed and taken into account. It's up to you to define "by whom" or "by what." Do the specifics really matter when you're in a place like this?

We're nearing the halfway mark. How you doin'? We can stop anytime. You tell me. You're not talking much today. That's fine. Makes sense. I hardly ever talk when I'm here. It's something, though, someone'll always come along. They may ask a question or offer a comment, or sometimes it'll be me that does. I welcome that. It's a way for either of us to somehow express gratitude for being here in the first place. It wasn't the initial intention, but most of the time, it slips out while talking, "A stunning day, isn't it?" "Not too hot, not too cold. Just right." "Makes you feel grateful to be alive, doesn't it?" So many other things could have been said, but this is what ends up coming out. All the right things to say. All spontaneous, unscripted. For me, it's like church. But without prayer books and psalms.

You probably guess that about me already. Talking to strangers is one of my lessons. Being vulnerable again. You, too? Not everyone causes pain. Nature nurtures. Maybe that's why it's called Mother Nature. Meeting anyone in nature makes it all so much easier. Hey, I'm glad you're with me here today. You wanna sit? I don't mind at all. I do it once in a while. Quiet. There's only half a dozen benches up here, but every one faces the lake. The hilly part's coming up. You up for it? More foresty, too, closed in, with fewer vistas.

What's your favorite part so far? The big vistas? Or the part of the trail where the trees surround you? Maybe a mix is best. Kind of sounds like life, but I prefer vistas, being able to look out in a variety of directions, free. These trees are incredible, but they're all over the place here. Hope I don't take them for granted. Do you? Hear that? Highway noise. We're three-quarters done 'til we're back where we started. All the way around the lake. More vistas are on the way. Hope I haven't been talking too much. Soon, I won't say anything. I'll let you absorb it all. Easier for you to take home, to take it all with you, this memory, with as few distractions as possible. You, me, and nature. Kind of presumptuous to think this was all made for us. Fair to say that it was made for us all, everyone, all living things. None better, none more important than the other. Nature lovers of every kind. Even ants and mosquitoes. If they've got lessons too, I'll be damned if I'd know what they are.

Right around this bend, there's going to b—Oh, right. Shhhhhh. I'll let you be. Time to absorb unobstructed. Time for me to convey the biggest thank you I'm possible of putting together to—right. Shhhhhh. I'll do it silently.

"Thanks for this perfect time. Thanks for creating something so incredibly perfect. Thanks for introducing me to what I believe to be the best life has to offer. As long as I've been around, it don't get any better than this. This is the pinnacle of life and what it's all about. A raging success to have learned this long ago; never will I take any of what life has to offer for granted.

More than anything, thanks for giving me someone special to share this with today. Experts say that you're the sum of the five people you surround yourself with. Five?! I can't imagine that many. Although I may never see them again, thanks for giving me just this one. They proved that good people do lift you up. Hope I was able to do the same for them. During this hour or so, I made a new friend, and I'm grateful. Hope they liked all this as much as I did. Maybe it's too simple for them. Maybe they won't see it the way I do. Doesn't matter. That's what makes the world go 'round, doesn't it? Differences. Lessons. Different ways of expressing ourselves and learning from those different ways, different people. Maybe next time, I'll try to express my thanks in German. That's a different way, for sure. Frau Volkmann would be so proud. Ja wohl.

In English for the moment, thanks for this miracle."

Piece of Cake

At this stage of life, we're all in the senior class. It took work to get here, for sure. And you don't get to be a senior without having been a junior, sophomore, freshman, and all that comes before. All your required classes have been completed, and you've passed them all. Right now, you know why you're here; that's a given. It should be a no-brainer when waking up in the mornings now; first thing, be grateful for it all. And after that, you'll know that lessons are served to you on your breakfast plate, as they always were. At lunchtime, some new ones may arrive. But, these are all givens.

Now that we know, what's left? What's new? What's next? Choices. All those things that bring us pleasure. That make us feel good. Things we want to achieve, do, and make happen. Once we know our required courses, we're free to single out what we really want. Lessons were chosen for us specifically. We pick the rest. Both, really, are just as important. They're just about equal. Which is more significant to you? The cake? Or the icing that's on it? Another way to look at it is that life without free will would be too rigid. Too inflexible.

By now, you know a ton. Main lesson learned: you know you're already living your purpose, and that's why you remain here. Fully accountable for all. You choose to learn as you go along. You always have the option to not. Lessons grow in prominence and come up much more frequently when they're deliberately unlearned. Best to respect your lessons as you did your former teachers in school.

What are some of your electives in life? Do you have a to-do list? A bucket list? Now that you recognize yourself as an undeniable success, what else is going on? Life certainly is a lot like school, ain't it? I mean, isn't it? It's filled with options, but the most unavoidable is to learn or not to learn.

As we grow older, it may be natural that our ability to

remember *everything* fades. It's difficult to gauge if what you still remember is more important than what you no longer do, but never forget your lessons. Too costly. And now, you're at the stage of life when time's balance sheet no longer is.

Maturity has taught you better. Taught us better. Right? Taking responsibility is a mature action. Blaming others when *you're* responsible is immature. Something children do. How lucky you are, though: living life, making decisions, taking responsibility now as a mature, wise adult while honoring the kid inside you that lives for little more than fun and games. Kids love both, and you should need no convincing that there's a child living within you. They remain alive as long as you do. They're innocent and have purity of soul. They're uncorrupt and see infinite possibilities. Live the rest of your life with this child within you, ever present in your adult life. Why not?

Are you up for some fun? There are so many different definitions of it. Either way, you deserve it. You deserve it if you've chosen to learn your lessons, deserve it if you learn none, and deserve it if you don't believe in lessons. Everyone's earned free time. It's available to all. What's your full life? Wow. That's a loaded question. Depends on how you see it. Is your life half full? Or half empty? Oops, another math question—let's not go there. Now that you're retired, you're at liberty to live your full life with more balance. Less stress, take it easy, and more than all else, know that your worth is based on who you are vs. what you've achieved and accomplished (in the material world or not).

I'm not rushing you, but get busy livin' or get busy... Well, you know the rest. Take responsibility for your life. If you've lived with injustice, make it right! Learn from it and be grateful for your new beginning. Choose to keep your tank full because your motor's still runnin'. Your choice. When you let your tank run low, excuses take over. No time, no energy for this or that. We're too old to rely on excuses for anything.

Every day, we're given a multitude of chances. To learn, to experience, and more than all else, to begin again. It should be a given, but when given a new chance at anything, be grateful for it. Even for what you may have felt is miniscule. Try not to forget that when you're grateful, you get more. When you're not, you get nothin'. And always recall those times when you had none.

Fulfillment and Satisfaction

Feel all those great feelings that come from your hard work. Take your mind back to your working life, similar to those diligent folks on the StairMaster at 24Hour Fitness in Cupertino. Hard at it, determined, motivated, self-believing, knowing that they deserve every reward for all the goals they made real. Like them, my wish for you is that you take your work ethic with you upon retirement. What a great life that's going to be to transfer all that positive momentum and belief to lesson learning (if you're not already doing so). Some folks are capable of both living life's purpose *and* achieving and accomplishing at the same time. Whether you've got their drive or a fraction thereof, continue to work your true purpose with fervor. You're going to feel so fulfilled and satisfied when you do.

Another feeling that's worth mentioning is forgiveness. Go easy. Go easier. Forgive *yourself* for not being perfect, for not having achieved what you thought you were meant to (if you haven't). Know that one of the big reasons for not having is because you were meant for other things instead. Meant-to-be's are—for the most part—out of our control. Let it go.

The same goes for mistakes and regrets. They happen. Mistakes are often directly related to lessons. Accept, forgive. We're here to learn, your older self in particular. Yes, we're here for lessons, but we're here for a host of other things, too.

Short-term fixes are the same as no fixes. No lessons learned. Procrastination is fine; it means you're not quite ready. But it doesn't mean that you're never ready. Avoidance is not meant to be. It's 100 percent on you. You know your lessons and what you need to work on. Learn them. It gets better. Feeling calm and peace from within is a great place to be.

Feel gratitude for your longevity. Feel thankful that you've earned retirement. Feeling grateful yields one of the biggest rewards: it makes you realize how rich you are. It turns it all around. You've gone from lack to surplus within the blink of an eye, all in your mind. Each task mastered = fewer repeats.

How are you feeling? I hope you're in a good place right now. This could be the most fulfilling time of your life. You've earned this. You're wise because of what you've chosen to learn. You can be born with intelligence; nurture it, grow it. Intelligence is something you can learn in your life. Wisdom is something you acquire from having learned. Have you ever met anyone who was *born* wise? There are old souls out there; maybe they were born like that. Who knows? It doesn't mean they have fewer or more lessons than the rest of us. Lessons are meant for all, even those most wise.

Bottom line: be yourself. Be brave enough to be your authentic self and let it show as often as possible. Don't be shy. You're giving the person in front of you a treat by exposing your full self. They're going to appreciate your fearlessness, your vulnerability. Maybe you'll inspire them at the same time. Maybe they'll return the favor. What a feeling! The most valuable exchange you're ever going to feel is two people who are not hiding a thing. Make the most of this interaction.

You already know what Ferris Bueller's up to, but what are you going to do on *your* day off? Days off? Ain't freedom a great thing? The liberty to do whatever you want, whenever you want. These are the rewards you've worked for and long deserved. Lessons keep you going, and on those days off in between, they make the life you're living more enjoyable. Bilanciata.

Now that you've been told a million times that you're a success, are you enthused about what's to come? You've grasped hope, acceptance, gratitude, and all those ingredients that make up a winner, including a new definition of "life's purpose." Enthusiasm means an intense enjoyment one brings to the table once they know "they got this." It's more than hope, optimism, and fun. You gotta know for a fact that you got this thing called life. You know this now. It's all about living your life's true purpose via the lessons you've been given. In a nutshell, *that's life!* Live and learn. You now clearly see the wisdom that's on your face every time you look into the mirror.

U.S. News & World Report observes that you may feel a range of emotions as you enter into retirement; four appear prominently, but excitement tops the list. It's only natural to feel a mix; you're only human, after all. Nervousness and curiosity are there. The fourth is relief.[26] Now that you've arrived, exhale and breathe! Time to celebrate that arrival with excitement and enthusiasm.

Enthusiasm is a word oftentimes associated with new beginnings. An enthusiastic new beginning, an enthusiastic fresh start. You all are so lucky and blessed to have the opportunity to begin again. Why not do it with enthusiasm?! No doubt about it, you've earned it. Time for you to do you, the new and improved one. Now that lesson learning has become second nature to you, go all out. Be outrageous (within reason)! Add items to your to-do list you never would have entertained before. And don't care if anyone else sees your list by accident. Remember, there's no such thing.

It's time to reintegrate the word fun into your life. And don't just go through the motions, either. It's time. Maybe you'll inspire others while doing so by showing them how much fun there is to be had.

You've got only one person to convince, though. Step back in front of your mirror and say, "I'll show you!" That's the only scripted line I'm giving you. You improvise the rest. Make your monologue as long or short as you want, but be certain to deliver it with enthusiasm. You know why? You've got an audience that wants to see how far you've come. Make it known. Make *yourself* known. Your *wiser* self.

Show Me!

Get enthusiastic about what's to come by demonstrating it. Nothing brings about change better than demonstration, evidence that you're ready. Like when Judge Judy yells out, "Show me!" You've been preparing all this time to have ultimate success, but all the prep in the world doesn't match real-time gameplay. Whether you believe in yourself 1,000 percent, you've still gotta show it. Let it be known. To anyone, anywhere, anytime. It doesn't matter if you believe in _____ or _____ or _____. Just let it be known that you're ready, you've changed, you've grown. You've done your work. And, most of all, you've learned your lessons.

Be intentional about this by doing even the smallest things differently. Do things that were not on the agenda. These distinct actions show that you're open to the new, the *what's next* and *what's to come*, no matter what time the clock displays.

When you're showing the world (or whomever/whatever) the real you, the new and improved you, the you that's been dying to come out, you're demonstrating what and who you deserve.

Finally. You won't settle for anything less. You deserve to get back exactly what you put out. If you don't get it back, you move on. If this makes others uncomfortable, let *them* move on. Don't expect them to change. Never expect anyone to change. With the million-and-one lessons out there, there's still going to be a million-and-one folks that believe none exist.

Justice is out there, but it won't manifest at all if you're not prepared to defend yourself. Make careful note: defending yourself is not the same thing as being defensive. If you believe in such a thing, don't expect karmic justice to take place just because you believe it should. Happens naturally? It may or may not. You're here; you're alive to do your part, be you fully, and show up 100 percent as often as possible. When Judge Judy asks, "Where'd you think you were coming today? To the beach?" it evokes laughter every time. Those poor fools that show up in court unprepared to defend themselves or prove guilt or responsibility have arrived there prepared to fail.

You're in a winning position once you realize there's something much greater than yourself out there assisting, guiding, and teaching you. I believe we are most certainly looked after. We're never empty. And things do happen for us at the right time. Yours is now.

If richness were measured by wisdom acquired, recognize your own name inside the *Forbes* Top Ten. You've earned that spot. This is how much I value lessons and their place in our lives. This is where I see myself; my name appearing on that list somewhere. Focus on what you have, what happened in your life vs. what didn't happen. Don't care what others think, and don't compare yourself to them.

You get it? You getting it? Sharing this with you now has been a pleasure. There are so many wishes I have for you, and I'm not kidding, but when thinking superlatives, my greatest wish for you is that you live your life with purpose. It doesn't matter if you see life as I do or if you agree that learning lessons is our real and true purpose. This is my view. I'm trying to make the point that living life isn't arbitrary. We're not here by accident, living these lives randomly. We all learn from each other. We all experience pain and suffering. No one is better than anyone else. I most certainly am not.

At 66, my life's better knowing how imperfect I am. It takes the pressure off. My ego's in check, and the only thing I keep inflated now are my tires. I not only have compassion for both my mom and dad, but I am grateful they gave me something tremendous to ~~do~~ learn in life. It made me appreciate the complexities—and simplicities—that go with it.

Go simple. Be simple. Accept and be grateful. Not just for lessons you've been provided with, be grateful for just being. It's the totality of others; your parents, friends, acquaintances, that person next to you on the StairMaster, that's the greatest gift. To learn from the totality of it all. Maybe their lives mirror yours, and you didn't even know it. What a gift it would be for you to influence someone else in a most positive and perhaps unexpected way. You've done something for someone else by merely being. You could be a tremendous inspiration to someone else and not even know it. Make your own personal universal every chance you get. Demonstrate it.

Leading by example gives our lives meaning. Become a person unafraid to learn any lesson that comes your way. Challenging? Yes. You already know that it cannot be done or learned overnight. You get that. Keeps you alive, for sure. Retirees or not, anyone of any age needs a reason to wake up in the morning. What's yours? Retirement doesn't mean you've become void of reason. It's a matter of seeing the reason differently. After you've re-defined it, it could be equal to or greater than your former reason for getting up. Everything is up to you.

Wisdom has no boundaries or limitations. Go for it all. I look forward to seeing your name soon on that Top Ten list. If yours happens to bump mine off, I'm cool with that. Show me!

TAKE ACTION

- *Assuming you've already identified your true purpose and you're living it, create and fill out a to-do list—free from purpose—and keep adding to it. Obligatory lessons were given to you at birth; now it's time for you to pick and choose what's optional. Everything you've always wanted to do. Pleasurable things, challenging things, satisfying things.*
- *At the very least, list five prominent, long-range activities that only a retired person is qualified to do, someone who's just graduated and has earned their degree (new to the "real world").*
- *Just as in years past, lessons will continue coming to you. They're going to happen anyway, so, in the meantime, keep learning, keep growing, and while you're at it...*
- *Give yourself a bear hug; you've made it this far! You're still here because...you're still learning!*
- *Have fun and enjoy life!*

Acknowledgments

God, You've provided the lessons of a lifetime and I'll always be grateful. Your creativity amazes me. Ever thought about a career in writing? Oh, that's right. Long ago You penned the most popular reality show in history. And it's still on. Good goin'.

Mom, without a good teacher, lessons are worthless. Thanks for being the best there is. Giving me life comes in second to the piece of your kind heart you placed inside it. Inherited directly from you. Genetics aside, I'll forever love and appreciate the totality of you.

Dad, that time we shared in Las Vegas was a bonanza. Decades of value condensed into a few days. There, I evidenced a good, intelligent, truth-filled man I was proud to call my father. Still do. Thanks for life, thanks for sharing your bravery.

Lia Ottaviano, hands down, no one knows how to work the English language like you. Saying that you're a true professional doesn't cut it. Thanks for your expert developmental edits, copy edit and for keeping my one-liners to a minimum. I'm no Henny Youngman.

Kam Bains, you're a standout! A very talented designer who innately knows compassion. It's been too easy working with you. People will continue to judge books by covers, so thanks for making mine a vivid, interpretative facsimile of the words I'd written inside it.

Lisa Highiet, are you kidding me with your loyalty? A lasting friendship that's going on five decades and counting. Thanks for not only this, but for your unbiased critique of early cover images. I swear, there's a reason so many of our lessons overlap, soulsista.

Darryl Jennings, Legal Counsel, and Michael Gross, Director of Legal Services at The Authors Guild. The legal expertise you shared re: permissions boosted my manuscript's authenticity. Thank you for taking the time to take me and my mission seriously.

Peter Parker, no doubt about it. You're one of the wisest souls I've ever met. I truly appreciate you, all you shared with me, your support and for seeing merit in *Revive Your Purpose*. This book was meant to take its place; hope it makes you smile.

Friends, acquaintances, loved ones, all living things from the past and present. Beyond grateful for the privilege of knowing you. The lessons I learned as a result of our connection was icing on the cake. Dark chocolate, of course.

The Honorable Judith Scheindlin, it's not possible to merely "watch" you on TV every day. You, *Judge Judy* and *Judy Justice* educate, make the legal system (and Judge Judy-isms) accessible to millions. You keep our hands clean. Thanks, teach. Thanks for the Yiddish lessons.

Shania Twain, Donny Osmond and Clint Black, you three have most certainly made your personal universal. Taking note of your stories helped me, made my life better. Your vulnerability is something I don't take for granted. Please keep sharing more.

Mama's Family, All in the Family, The Golden Girls, Roseanne, Friends, Dateline, The Tennis Channel, The Beverley Hillbillies, Get Smart, thanks for providing company, entertainment, and yes, even that occasional lesson that ends up lasting forever—for myself, for so many.

Rafael Nadal, no person will ever be able to copy your tennis talent, but thanks for inspiring everyone on the globe who knows you. IMO, you are its exemplar inhabitant. You prove that heroes ain't just for kids. Thanks for being mine.

Alice Walker, you not only write about those who suffer, you advocate for them. I'll gladly stand in line over and over again just to tell you "thanks" and see your smile once more. Until then…

Oprah Winfrey and Dr. Bruce Perry, what if everyone lived by your approach? Compassion would take over the world and all in it would be healed. Thanks for sharing such a wondrous insight.

24Hour Fitness, Cupertino, pedaling on the bike next to your StairMaster gave me a dream. Sorry for those days I went over 30:00 – hope no one else was waiting.

Notes

1. Rosenfeld, Jordan. "10 Surprising Stats About the State of Retirement in America." yahoo!finance, November 28, 2023. https://finance.yahoo.com/news/jaw-dropping-stats-state-retirement-200025720.html.

2. Searing, Linda. "More than 1 in 6 Americans Now 65 or Older as U.S. Continues Graying." The Washington Post, February 14, 2023. https://www.washingtonpost.com/wellness/2023/02/14/aging-boomers-more-older-americans/.

3. Steiner, Susie. "Top five regrets of the dying." The Guardian, February 1, 2012.
https://www.theguardian.com/lifeandstyle/2012/feb/01/top-five-regrets-of-the-dying.

4. Honigsbaum, Mark. "Barack Obama and the 'empathy deficit'." The Guardian, January 4, 2013.
https://www.theguardian.com/science/2013/jan/04/barack-obama-empathy-deficit.

5. Dogen, Sam. "What Age Do Most People Retire In America?" Financial Samurai, April 22, 2022.
https://www.financialsamurai.com/age-people-retire-america/#:~:text=According%20to%20the%20Life%20Insurance,have%20left%20the%20labor%20force.

6. Pawlowski, A. "How to live life without major regrets: 8 lessons from older Americans." TODAY.com, December 31, 2019. https://www.today.com/health/biggest-regrets-older-people-share-what-they-d-do-differently-t118918.

7. Docan-Morgan, Tony. "How often do people lie?" University of Wisconsin-La Crosse Blog, November 17, 2021. https://www.uwlax.edu/currents/how-often-do-people-lie/.

8. Vincent Mir, Heather. "Telling a Lie More Difficult for the Elderly." The Oldish®, November 27, 2018. https://theoldish.com/telling-a-lie-more-difficult-for-the-elderly/.

9. WebMD Editorial Contributors and C. Nicole Swiner, MD. "How Much Do You Shrink As You Age?" WebMD, April 7, 2023. https://www.webmd.com/healthy-aging/how-much-do-you-shrink-as-you-age.

10. Oaklander, Mandy. "Old People Are Happier Than People In Their 20s." Time, August 24, 2016. https://time.com/4464811/aging-happiness-stress-anxiety-depression/.

11. Digravio, Gina. "Optimists Live Longer." Boston University, August 26, 2019. https://www.bu.edu/articles/2019/optimists-live-longer/.

12. Williams, Bradley. "60+ Solo Travel Statistics (Latest 2023 Figures)." Dream Big Travel Far Blog, April 25, 2023. https://www.dreambigtravelfarblog.com/blog/solo-travel-statistics.

13. Hines, Kristi. "The History Of Social Media." Search Engine Journal, September 2, 2022. https://www.searchenginejournal.com/social-media-history/462643/.

14. Morrow-Howell, Nancy, Fengyan Tang, Song-iee Hong, Jaime Goldberg, So Yeon Kim, Amy Luman, Michael Sherraden, Amanda Moore McBride, Erin Auth, Kerry Finegan and Lisa Lawrence. "Older Adults in Service to Society." Washington University in St. Louis, Center for Social Development, Open Scholarship Institutional Repository, 2006. https://openscholarship.wustl.edu/cgi/viewcontent.cgi?article=1861&context=csd_research.

15. Bright, Jim. "What Do 1 in 3 people say about change? Some surprising stats!" LinkedIn, January 29, 2015. https://www.linkedin.com/pulse/what-do-1-3-people-say-change-some-surprising-stats-jim-bright.

16. Coxwell, Kathleen. "You Will Have a Happy Retirement and Other Fun Facts." NewRetirement, June 7, 2016. https://www.newretirement.com/retirement/you-will-have-a-happy-retirement/.

17. Wolchover, Natalie. "Will Humans Eventually All Look Like Brazilians?" yahoo!news, September 19, 2012. https://news.yahoo.com/humans-eventually-look-brazilians-140349518.html.

18. "Six Benefits of Practicing Gratitude for Seniors." Visiting Angels Sarasota, FL, n.d. https://www.visitingangels.com/sarasota/news-info/six-benefits-of-practicing-gratitude-for-seniors/16063.

19. Population Reference Bureau. "Countries With the Oldest Populations in the World." PRB, March 20, 2020. https://www.prb.org/resources/countries-with-the-oldest-populations-in-the-world/.

20. Good News Network. "70% Say They Always Trust Their Instinct, With Physical 'Gut Feeling' Used to Make Decisions, Says New Poll." Good News Network, June 18, 2022. https://www.goodnewsnetwork.org/70pt-say-they-always-trust-their-instinct-british-poll/.

21. McNeill, Brian. "For older adults, 'hope' may be a key piece for improving health, psychological and social well-being." VCU News, February 14, 2020. https://www.news.vcu.edu/article/For_older_adults_hope_may_be_a_key_piece_for_improving_health.

22. Reflections Management And Care. "The Importance of Keeping Hope as You Age: 5 Ways." Reflections Management And Care, Baldwinsville, NY, April 20, 2022. https://reflectionscny.com/the-importance-of-keeping-hope-as-you-age-5-ways/.

23. Smith, MA, Melinda, and Lawrence Robinson. "Sleep and Aging: Sleep Tips for Older Adults." HelpGuide.org, February 5, 2024. https://www.helpguide.org/articles/sleep/how-to-sleep-well-as-you-age.htm.

24. Pascale, Rob. "Why It's Important To Stay Social In Retirement And How To Do It." Forbes, October 31, 2019. https://www.forbes.com/sites/robpascale/2019/10/31/staying-social-in-retirement/.

25. Shmerling, MD, Robert H. "Right brain/left brain, right?" Harvard Health, March 24, 2022. https://www.health.harvard.edu/blog/right-brainleft-brain-right-2017082512222#:~:text=No%20evidence%20of%20%22sidedness%22%20was,than%20an%20anatomically%20accurate%20description.

26. Bernard, Dave. "4 Emotions New Retirees May Experience." U.S. News & World Report, January 16, 2015. https://money.usnews.com/money/blogs/on-retirement/2015/01/16/4-emotions-new-retirees-may-experience.

www.ingramcontent.com/pod-product-compliance
Lightning Source LLC
Chambersburg PA
CBHW020420010526
44118CB00010B/348